Firstly, I dedicate it to GOD, and families, where little artists of the heart and imagination, will color with all the affection. May pencils and paints be magical brushes, transforming this book into a vibrant universe full of life.

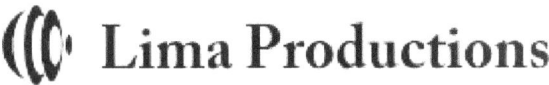 Lima Productions

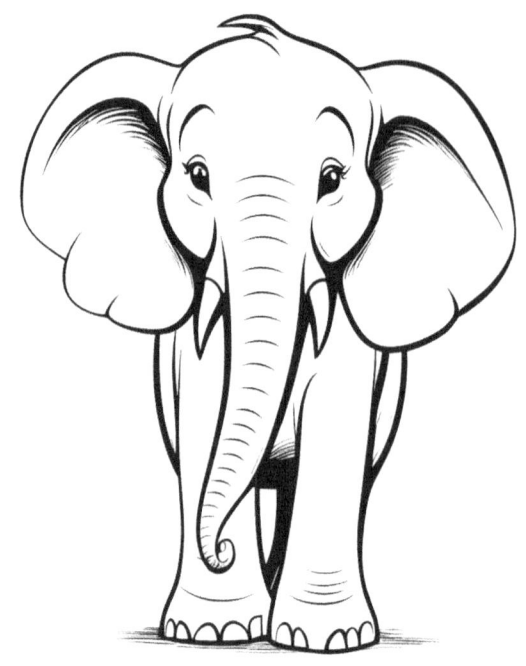

This Book Belongs To:

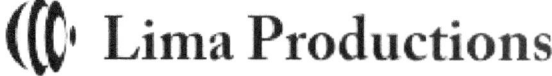

Lima Productions

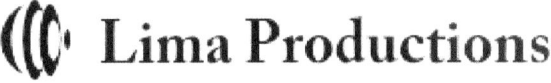 Lima Productions

Test Color Page

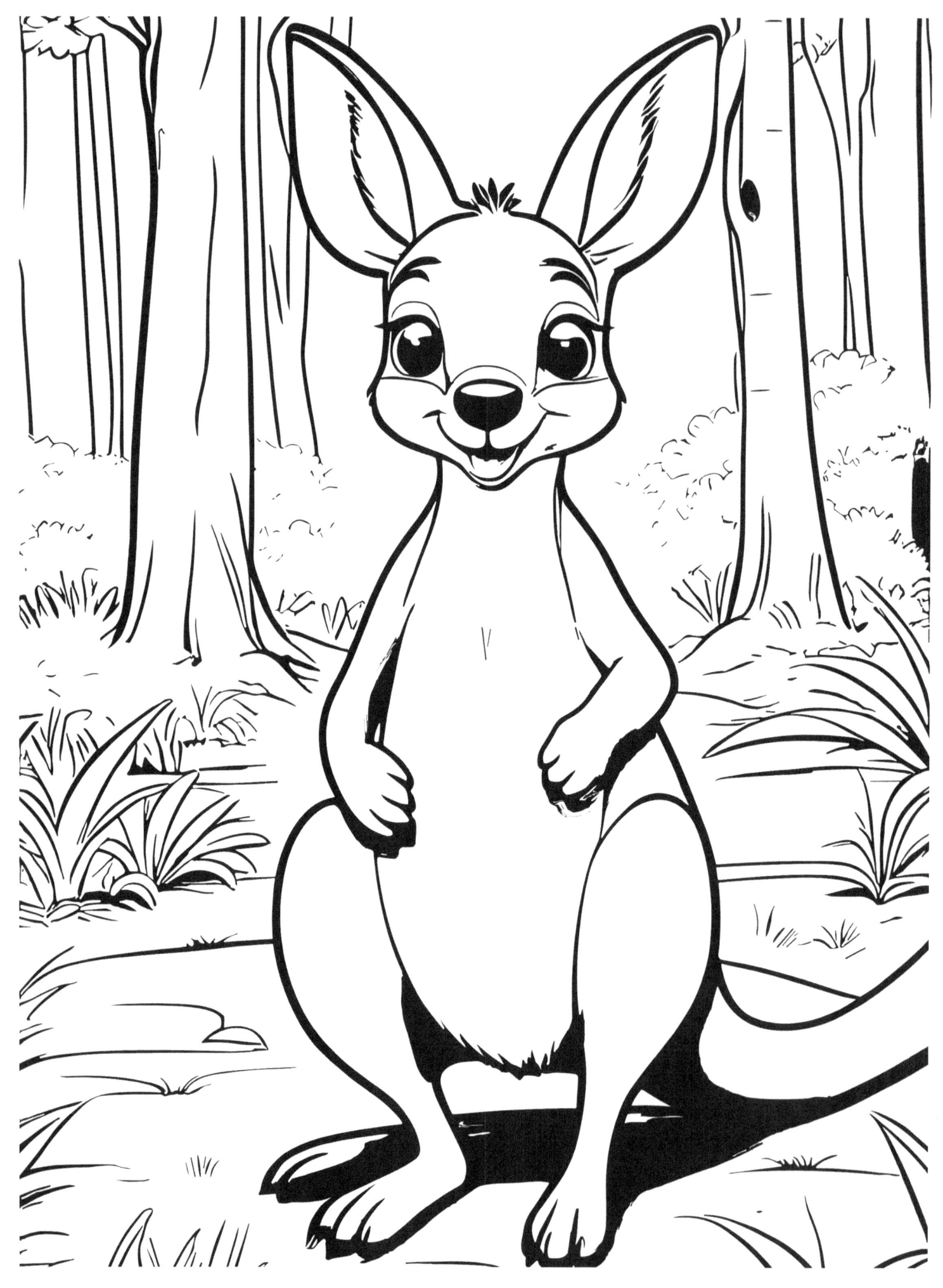

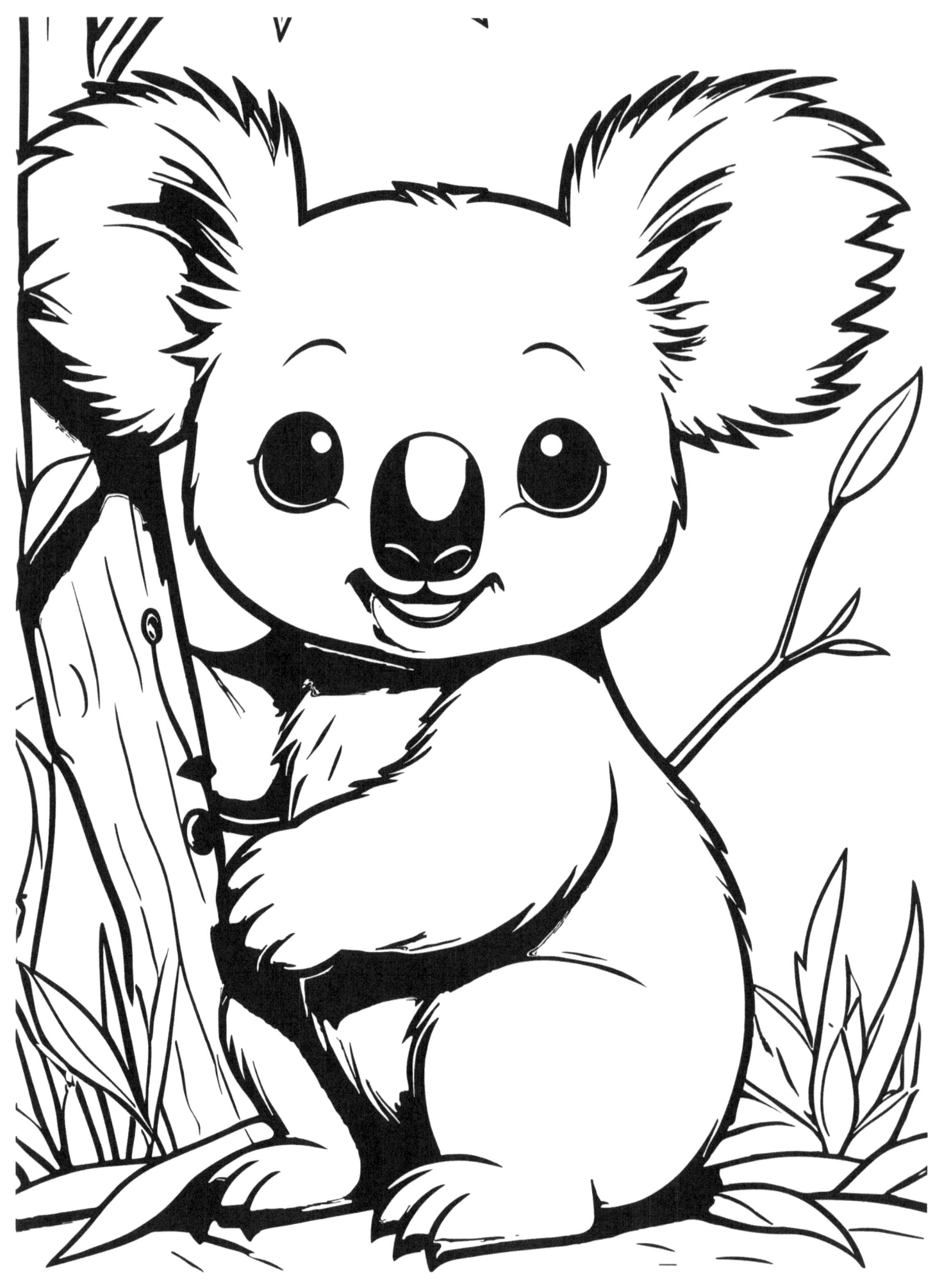

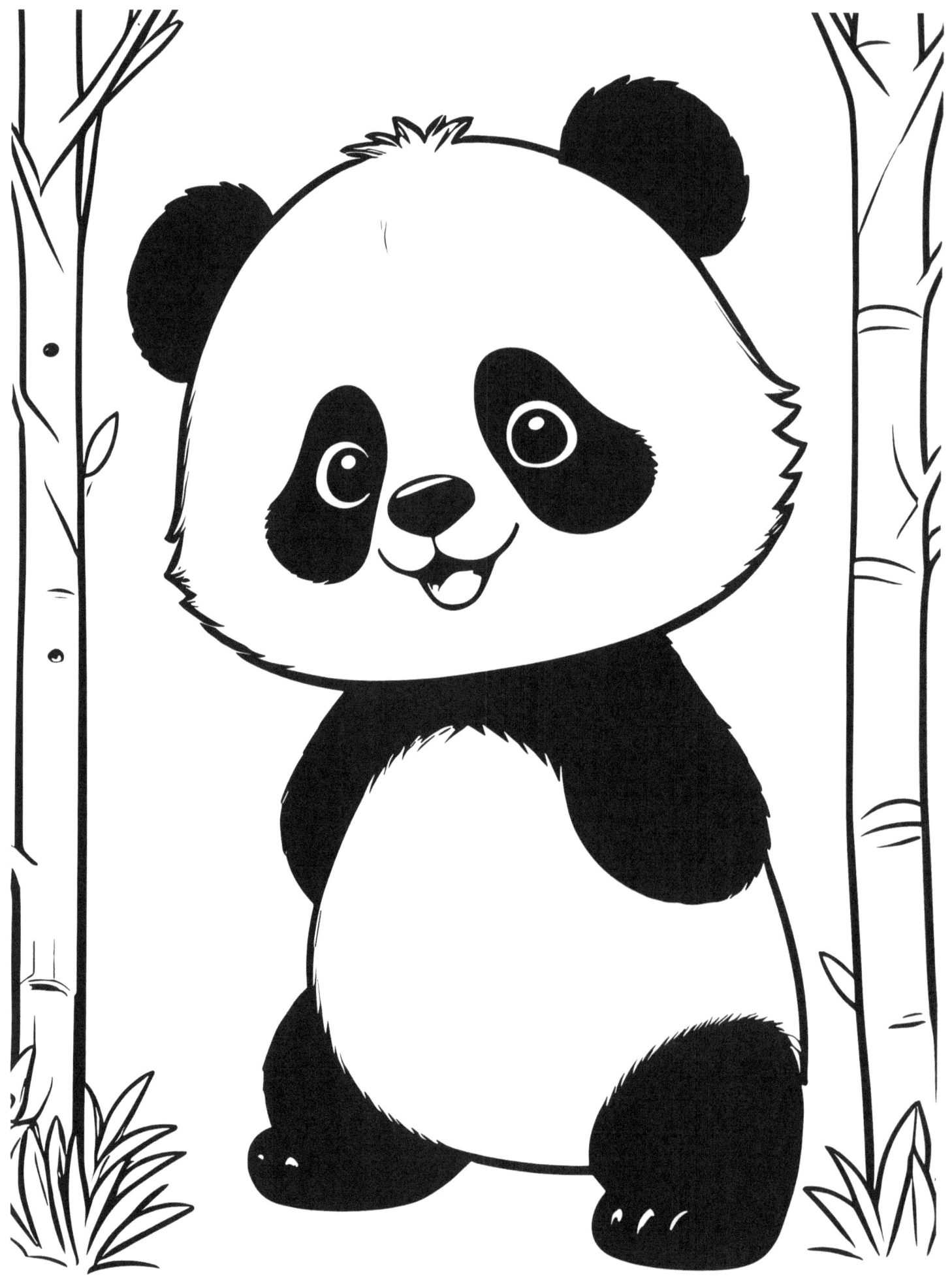

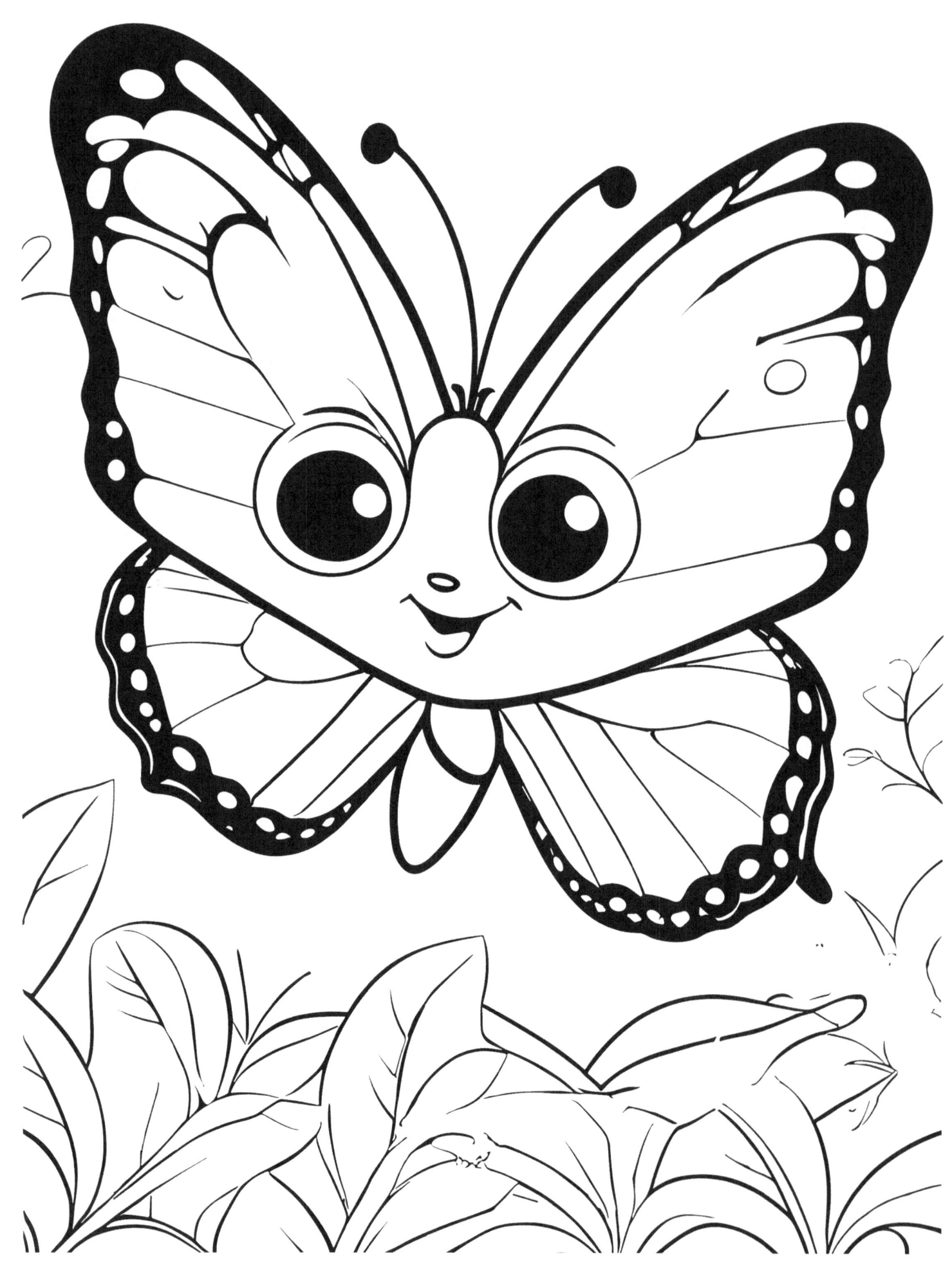

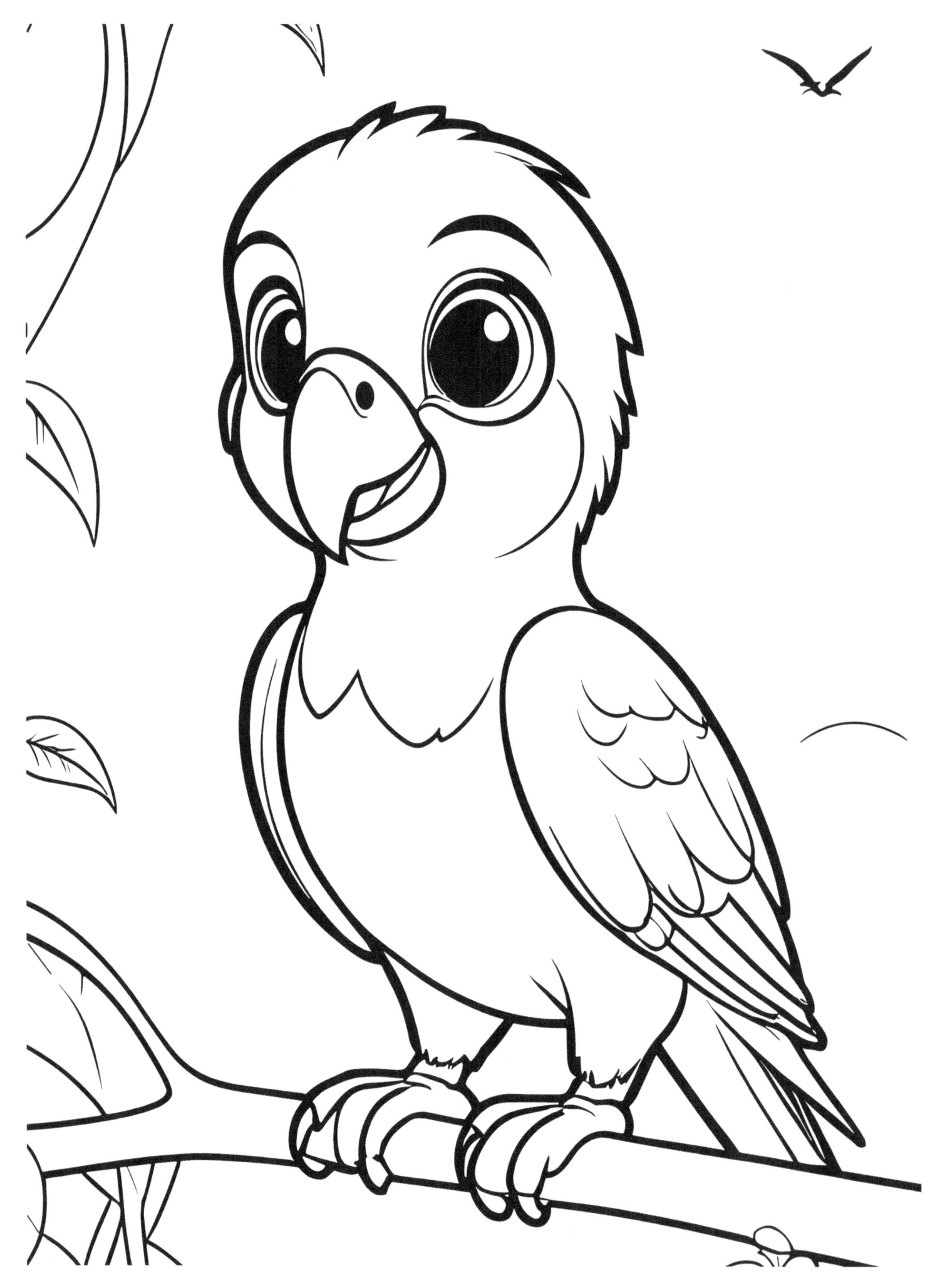

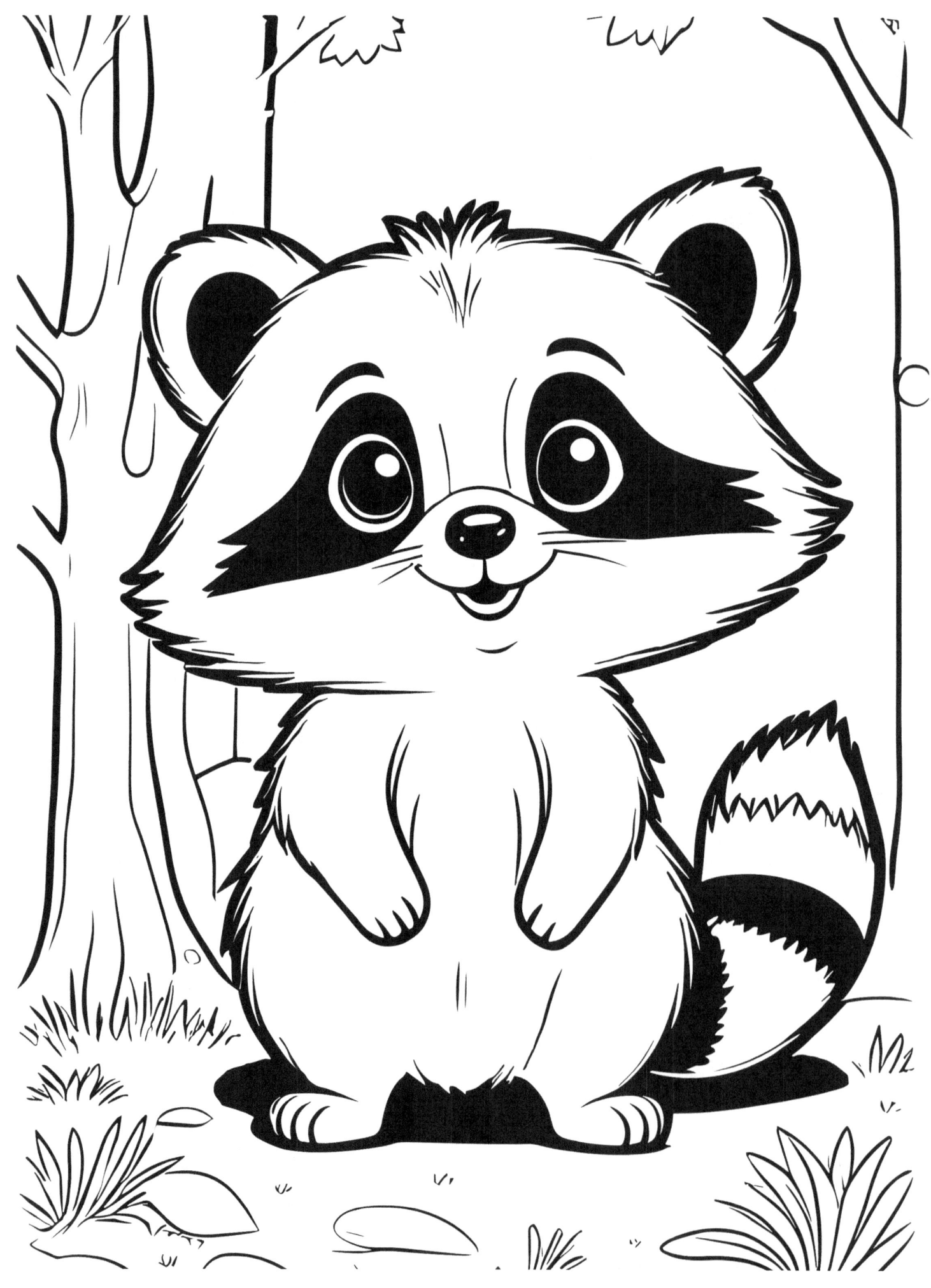

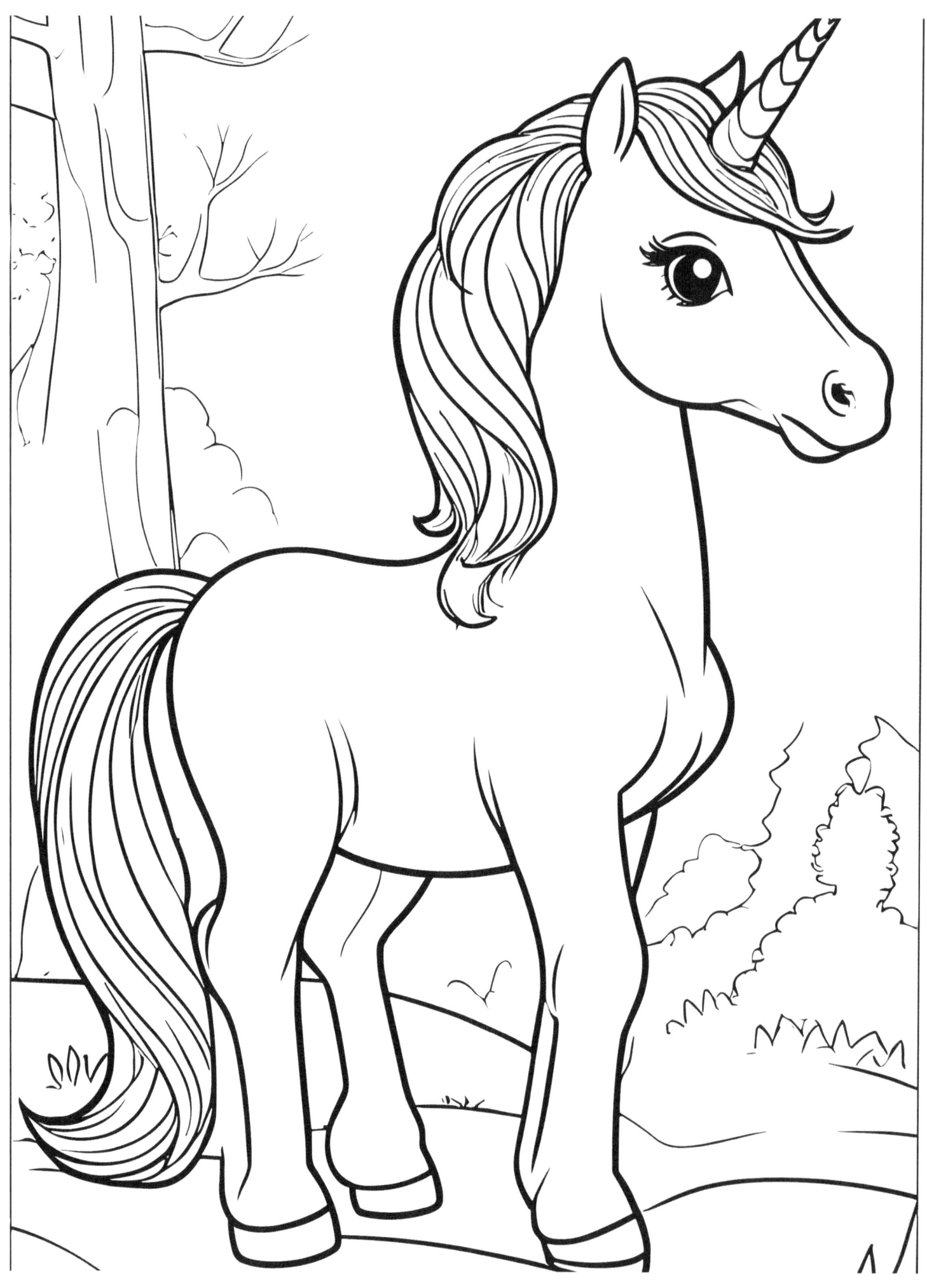

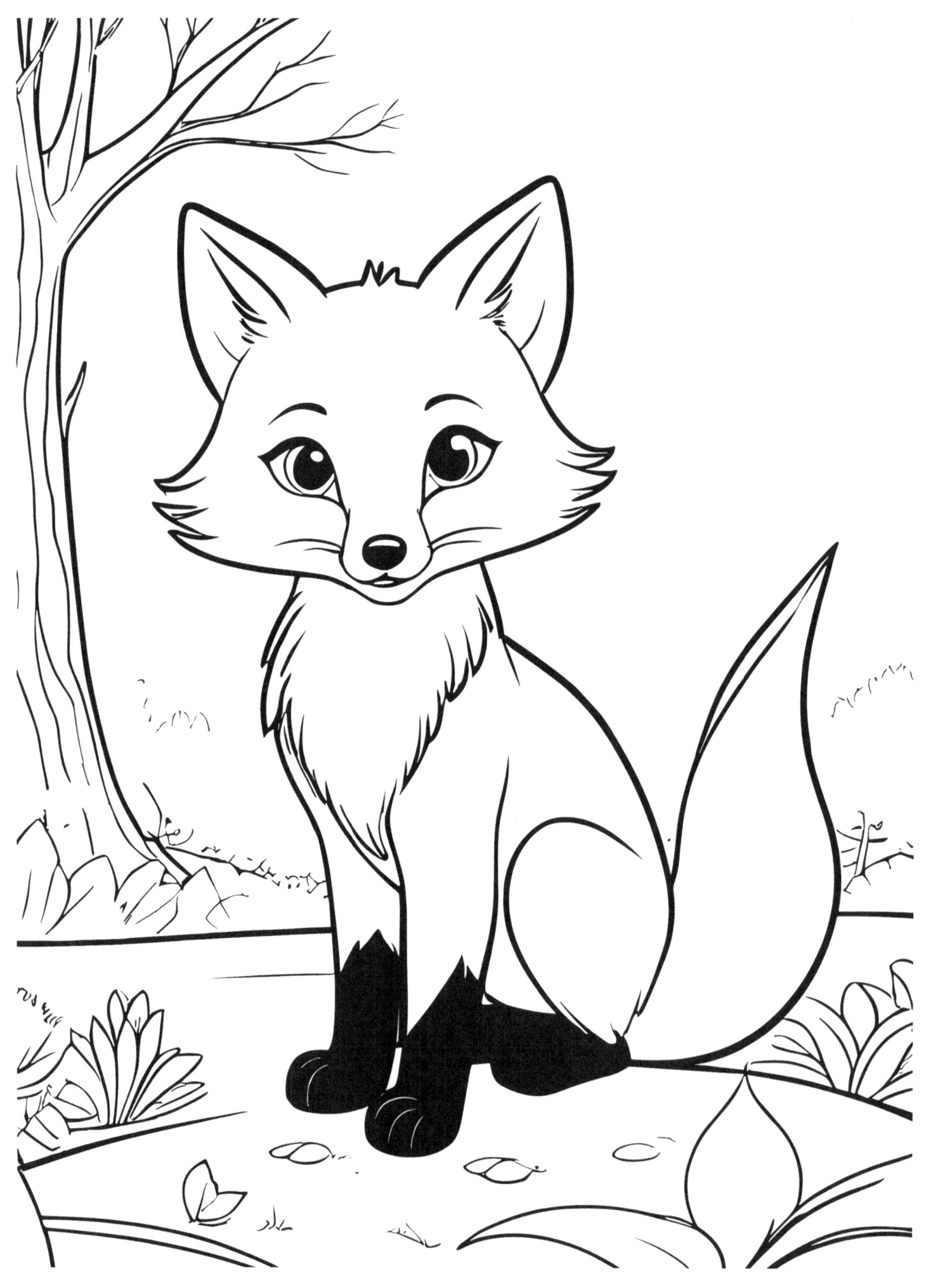

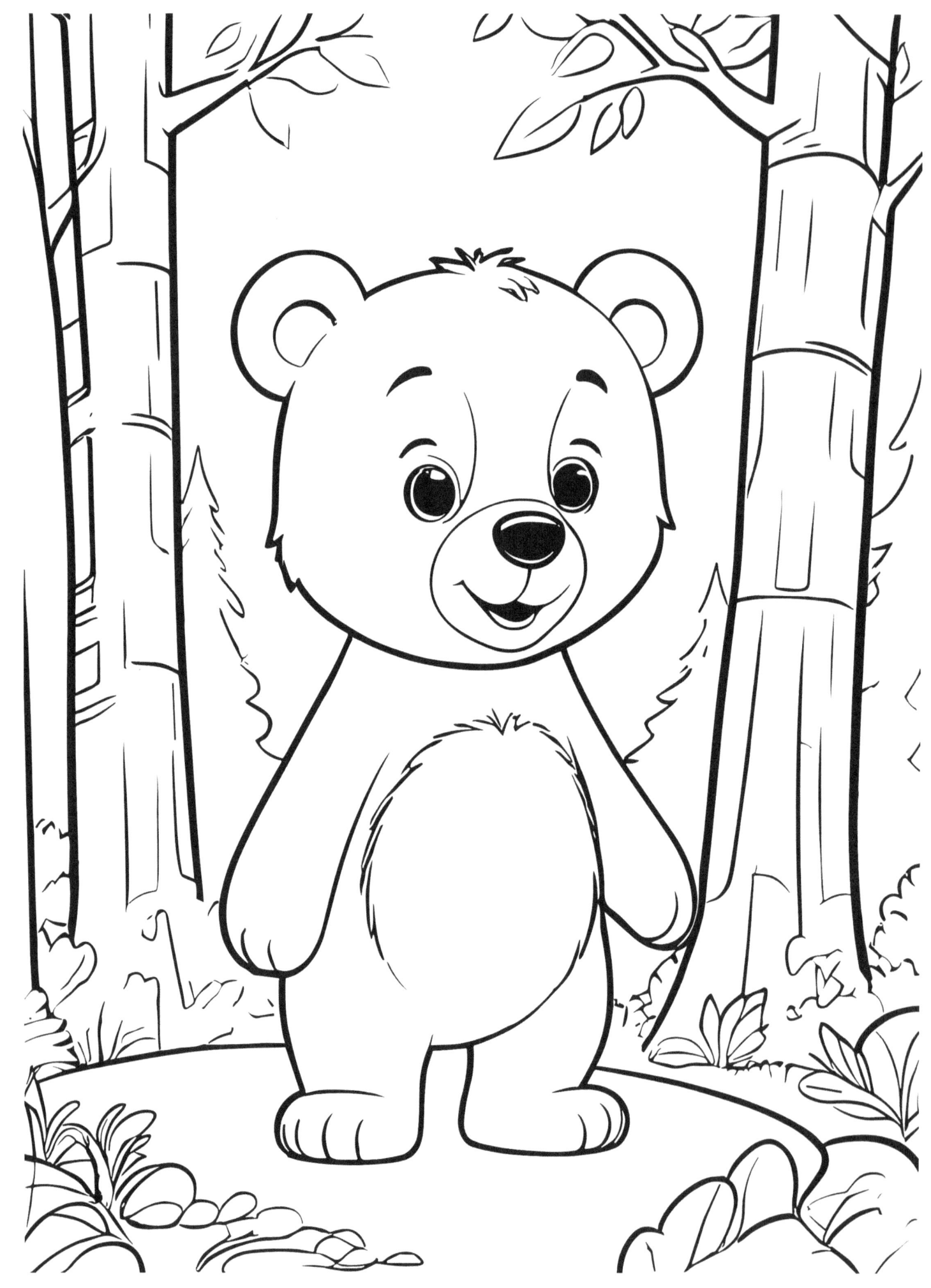

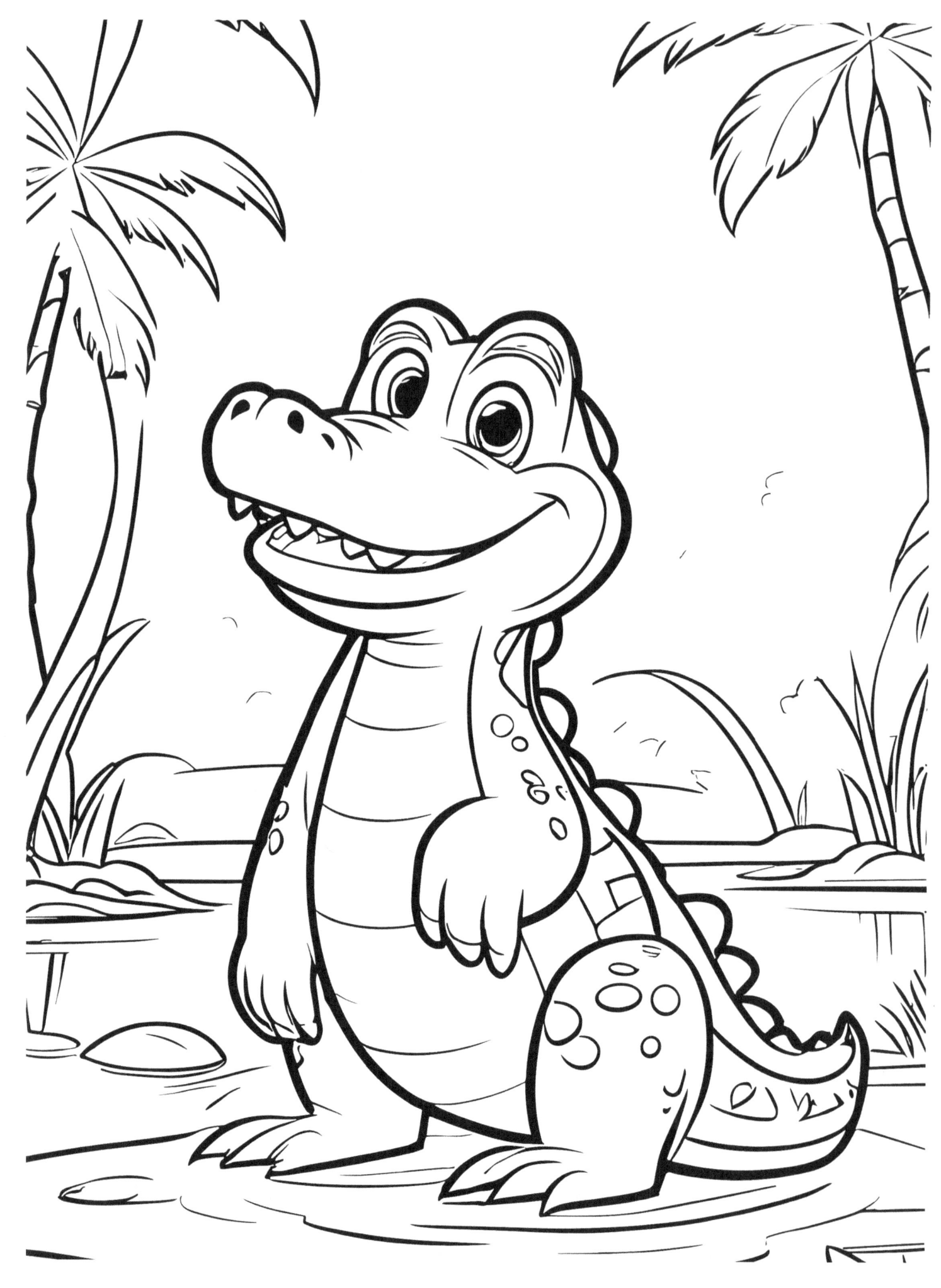

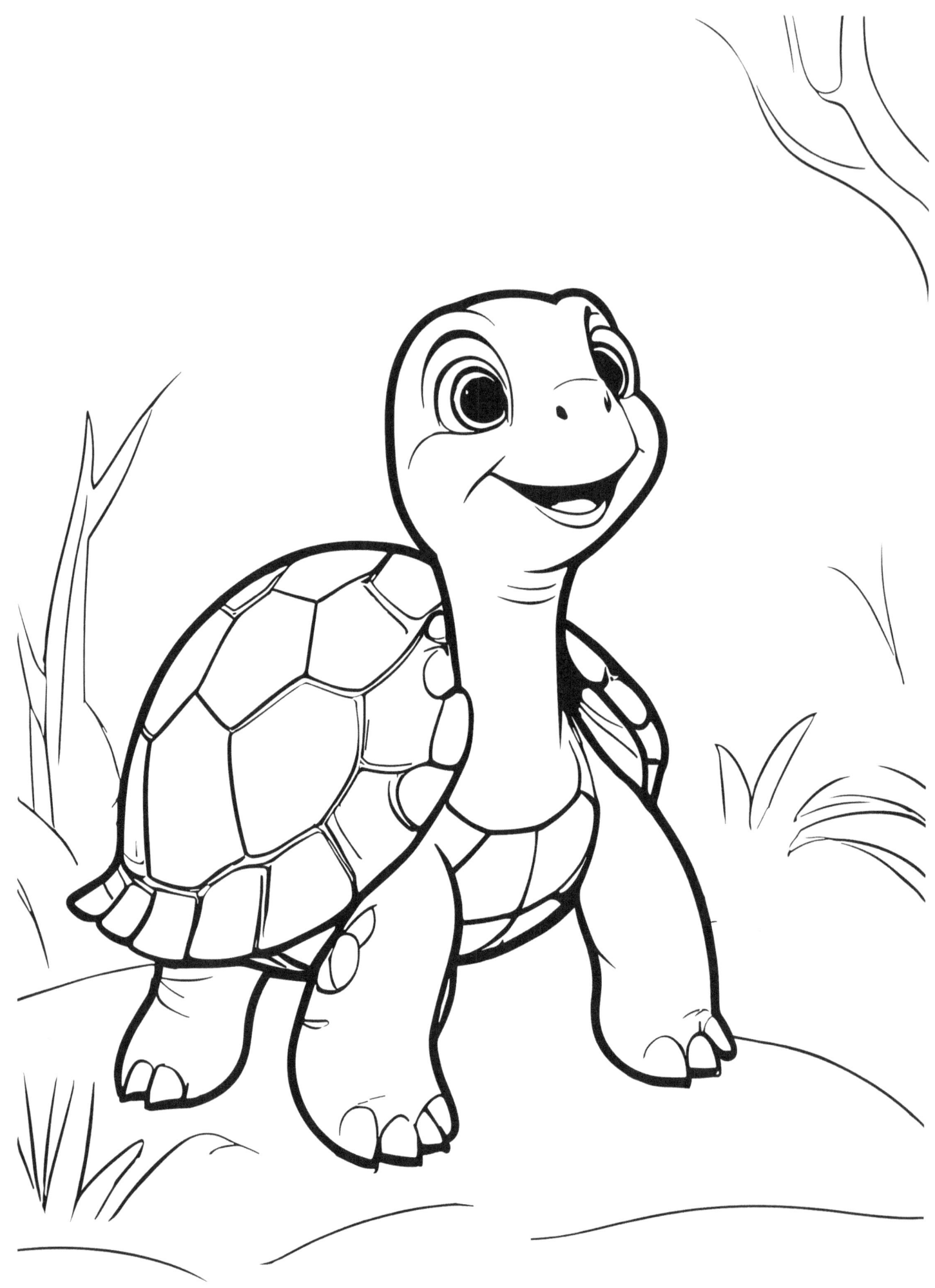

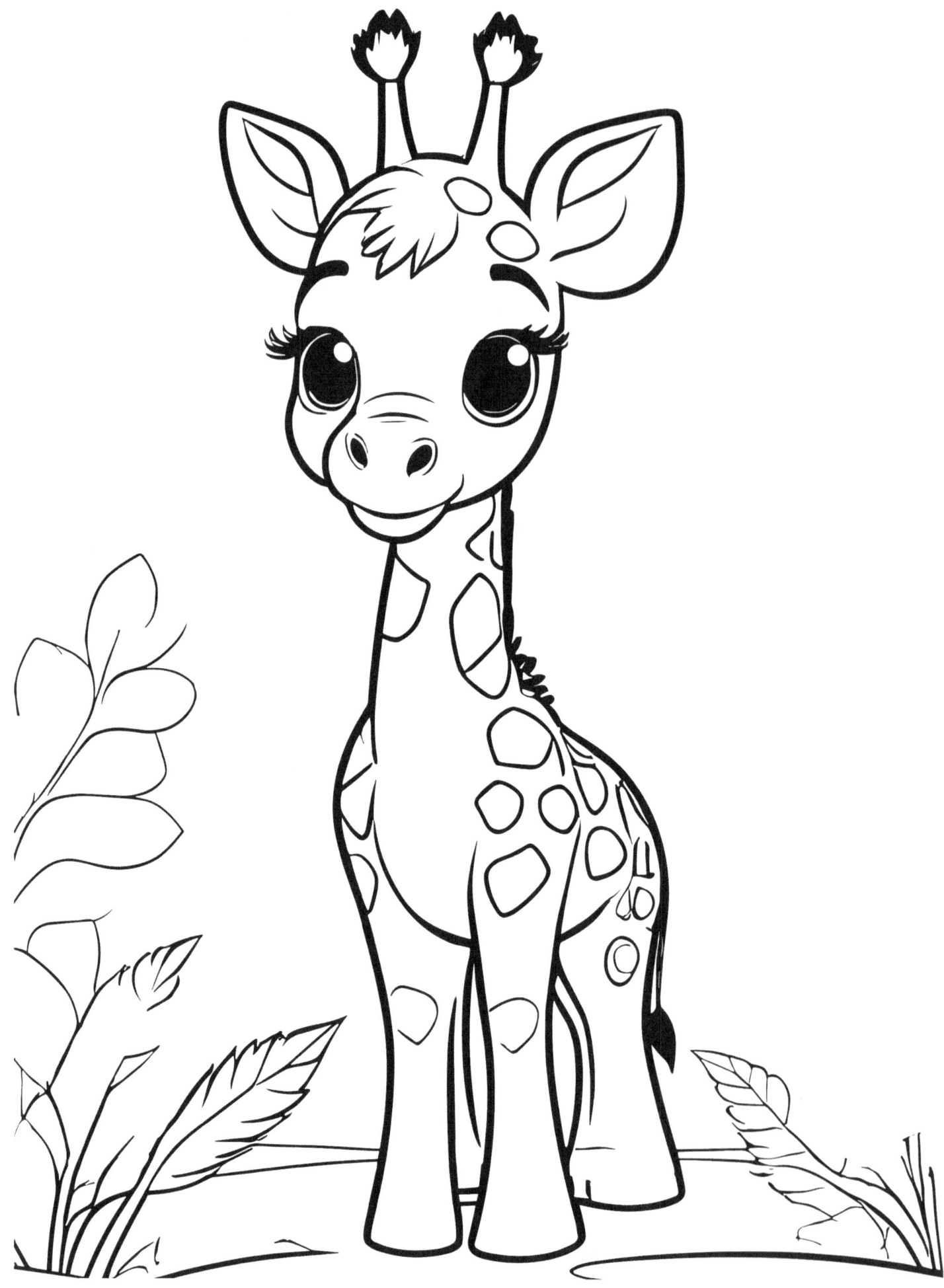

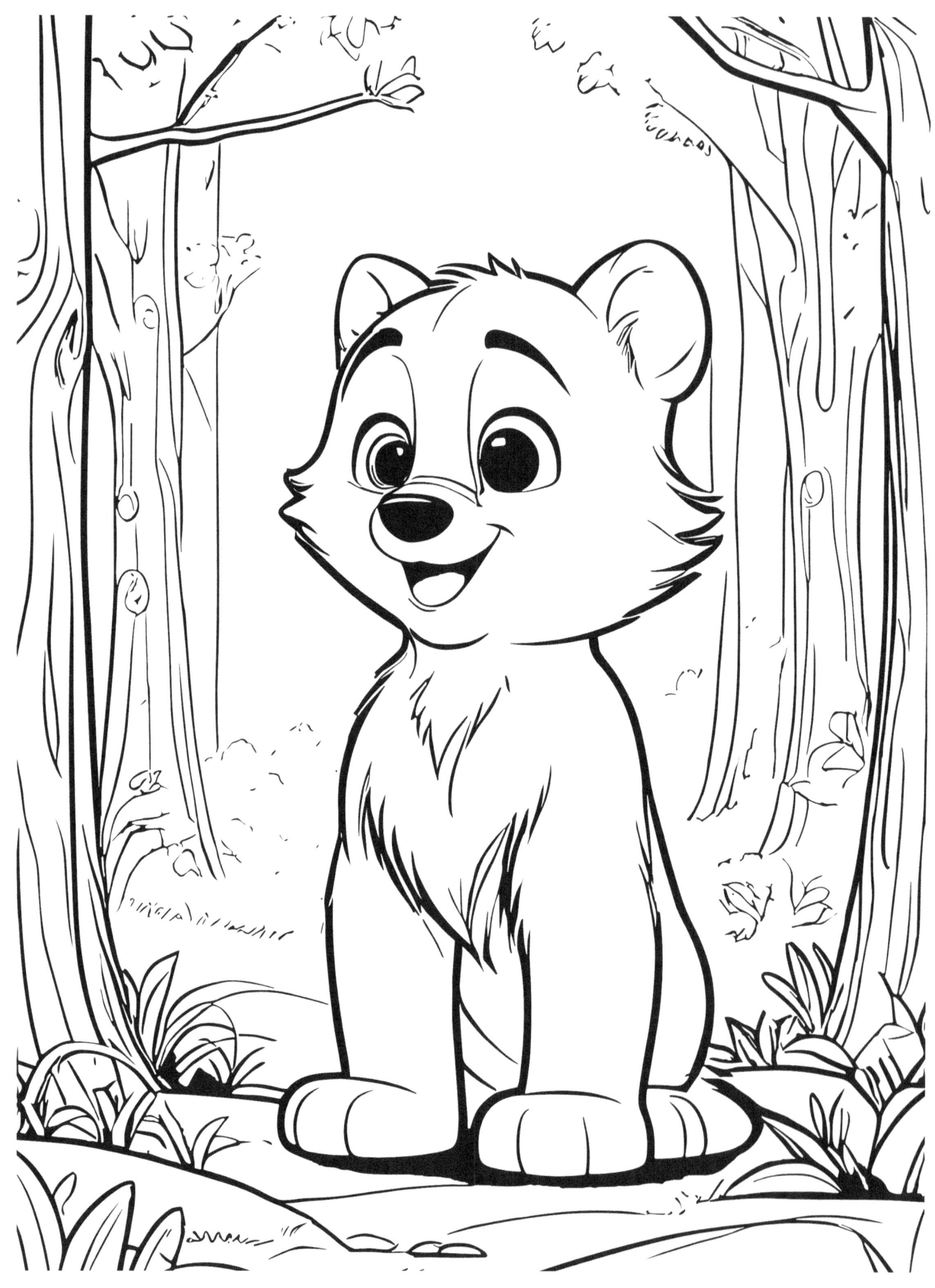

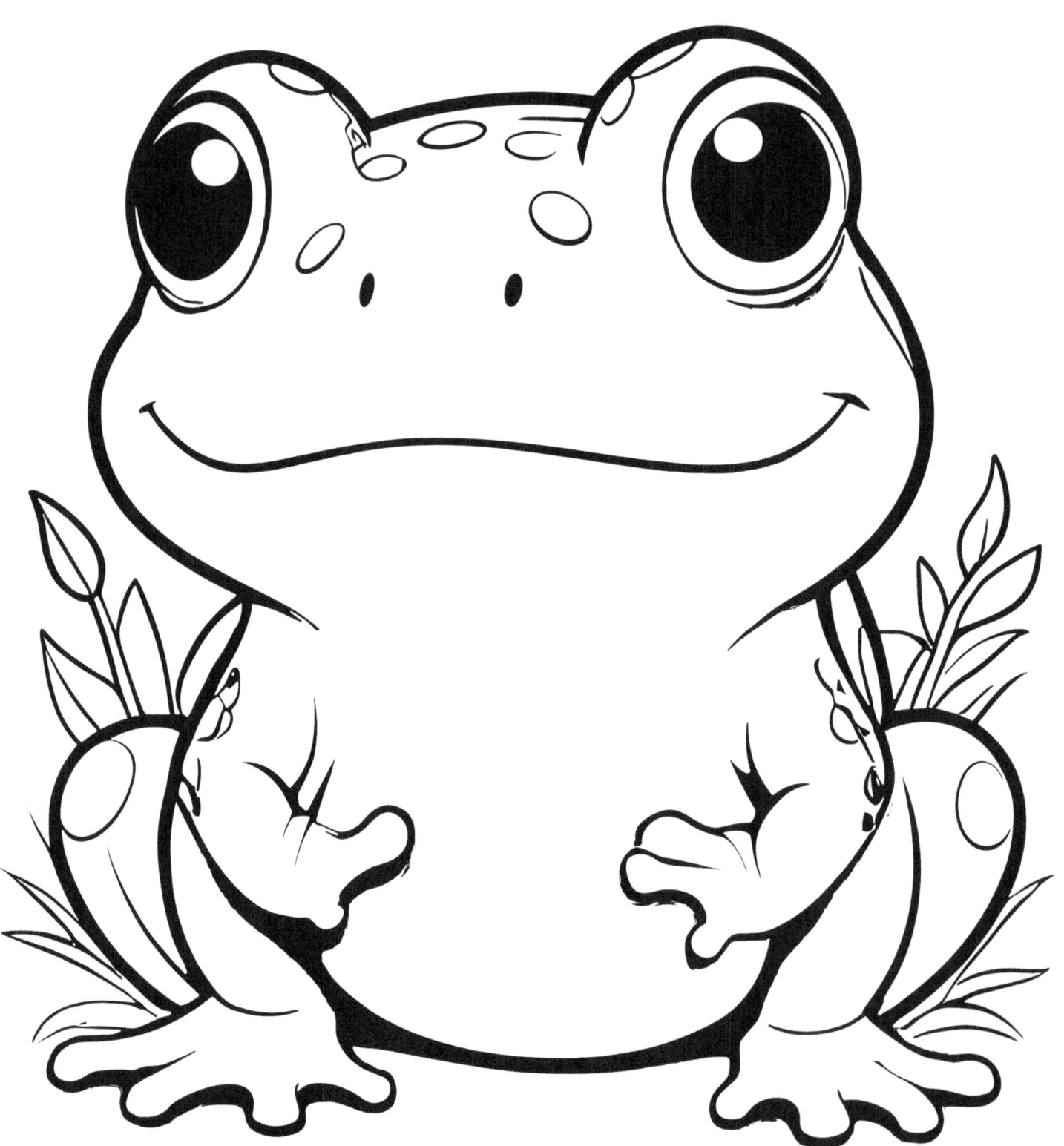

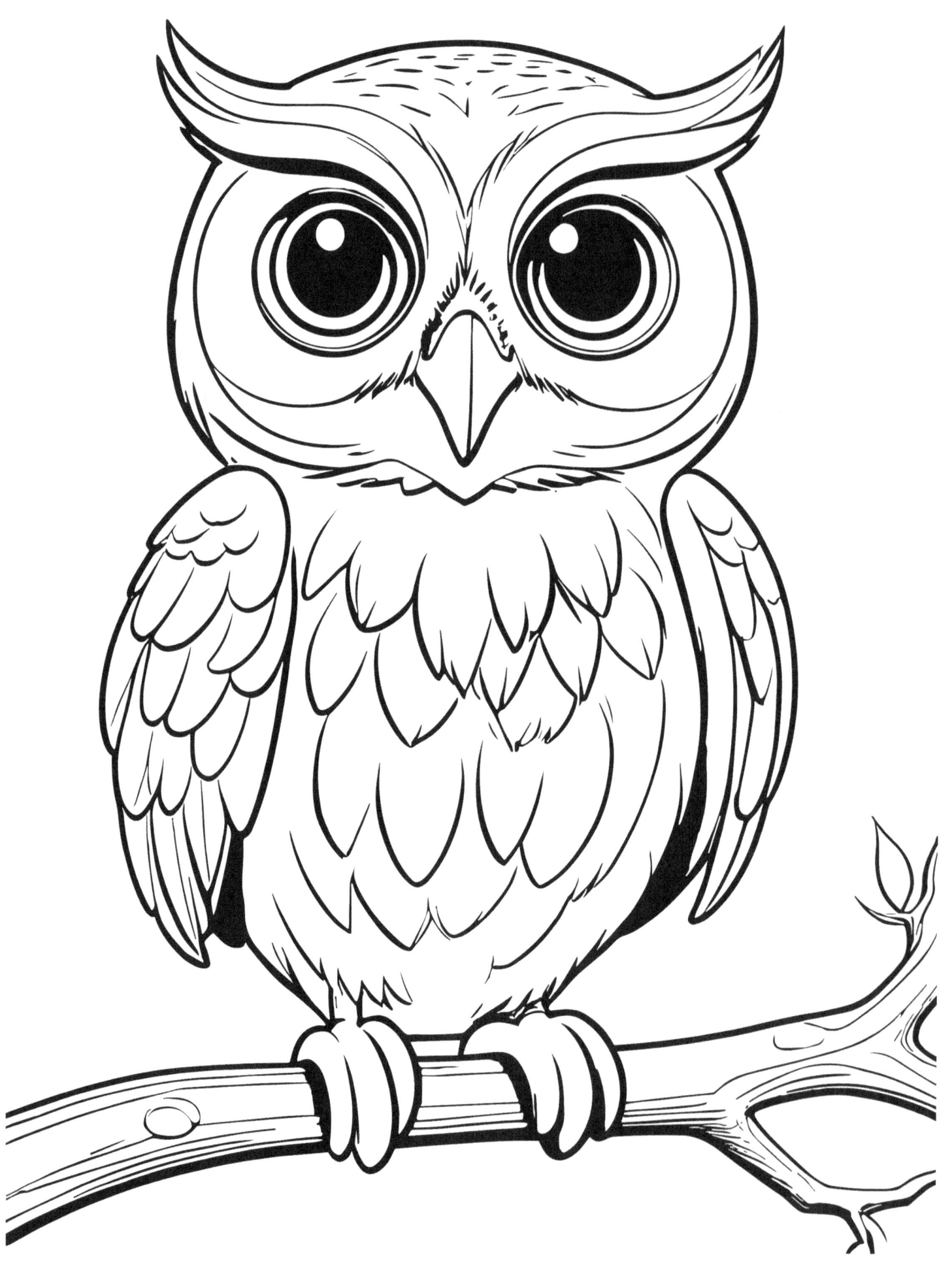

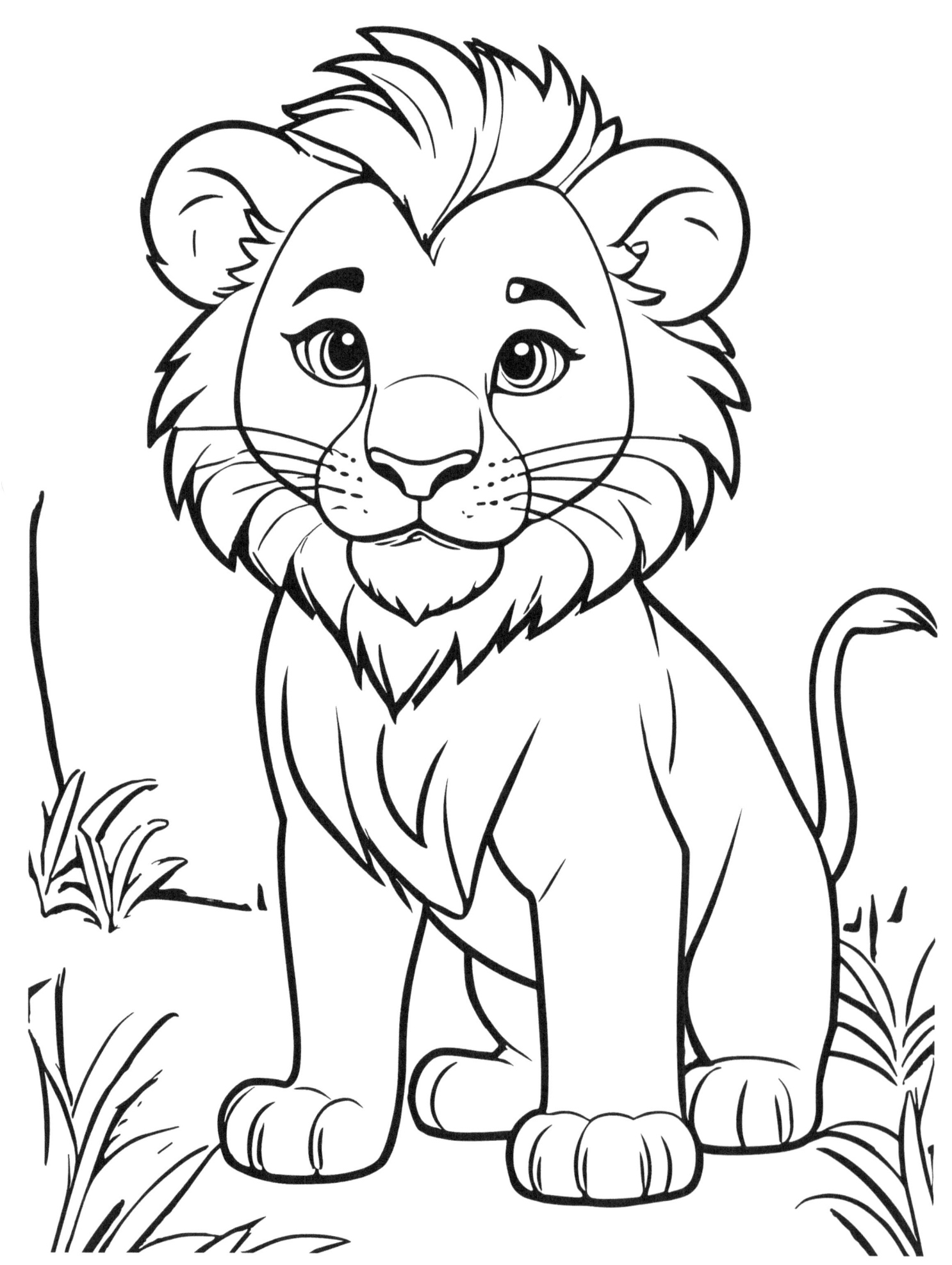

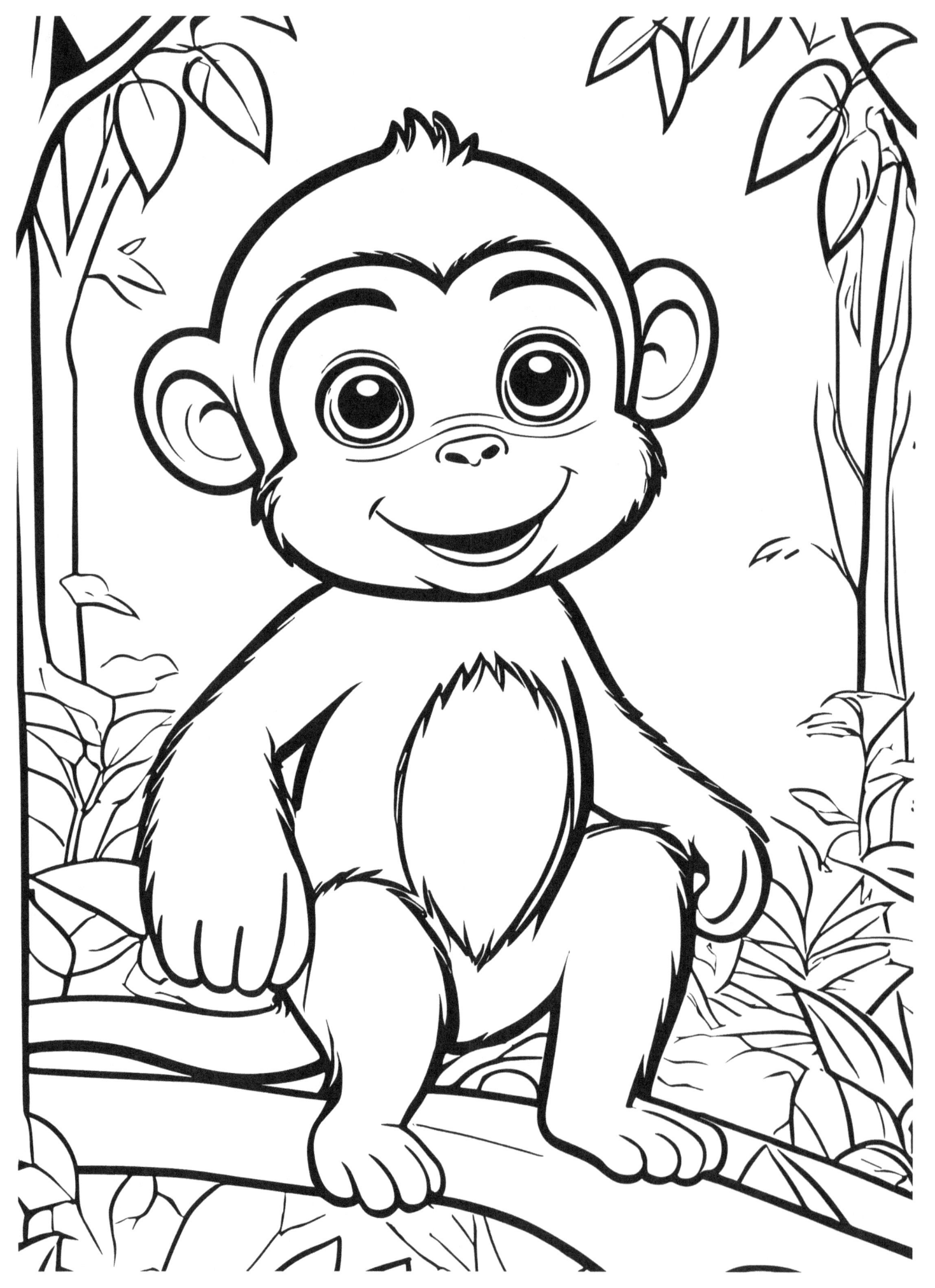

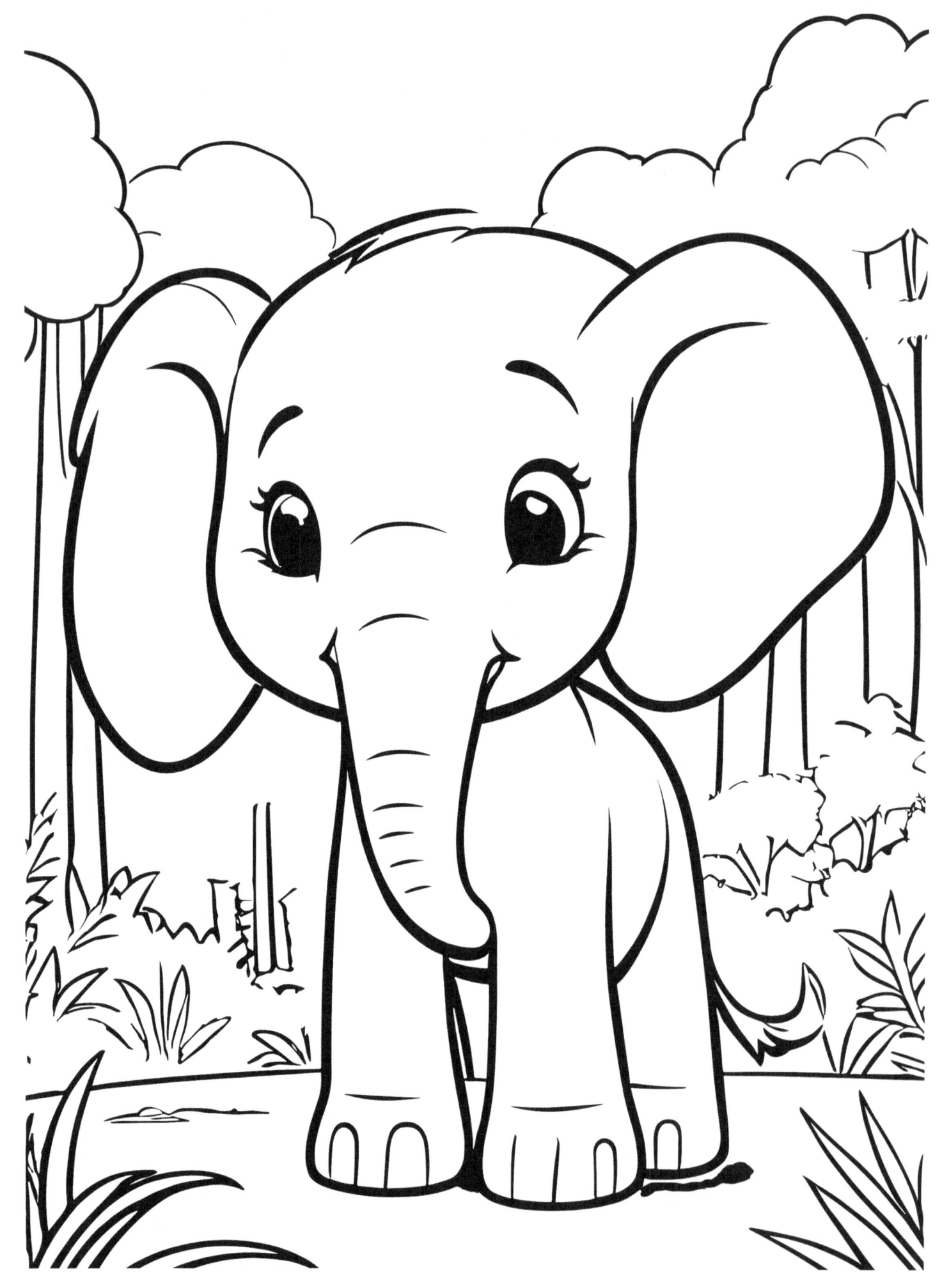

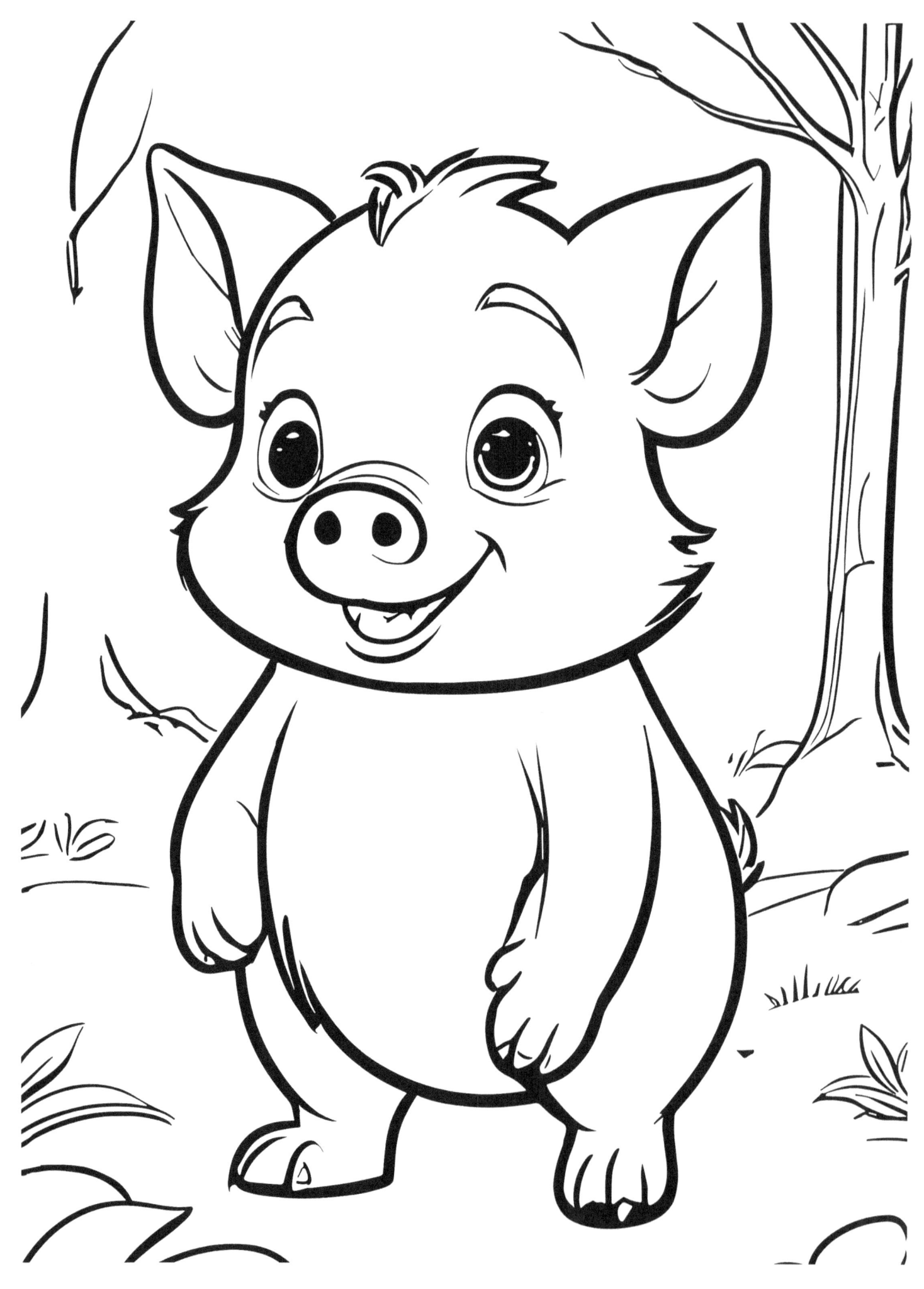

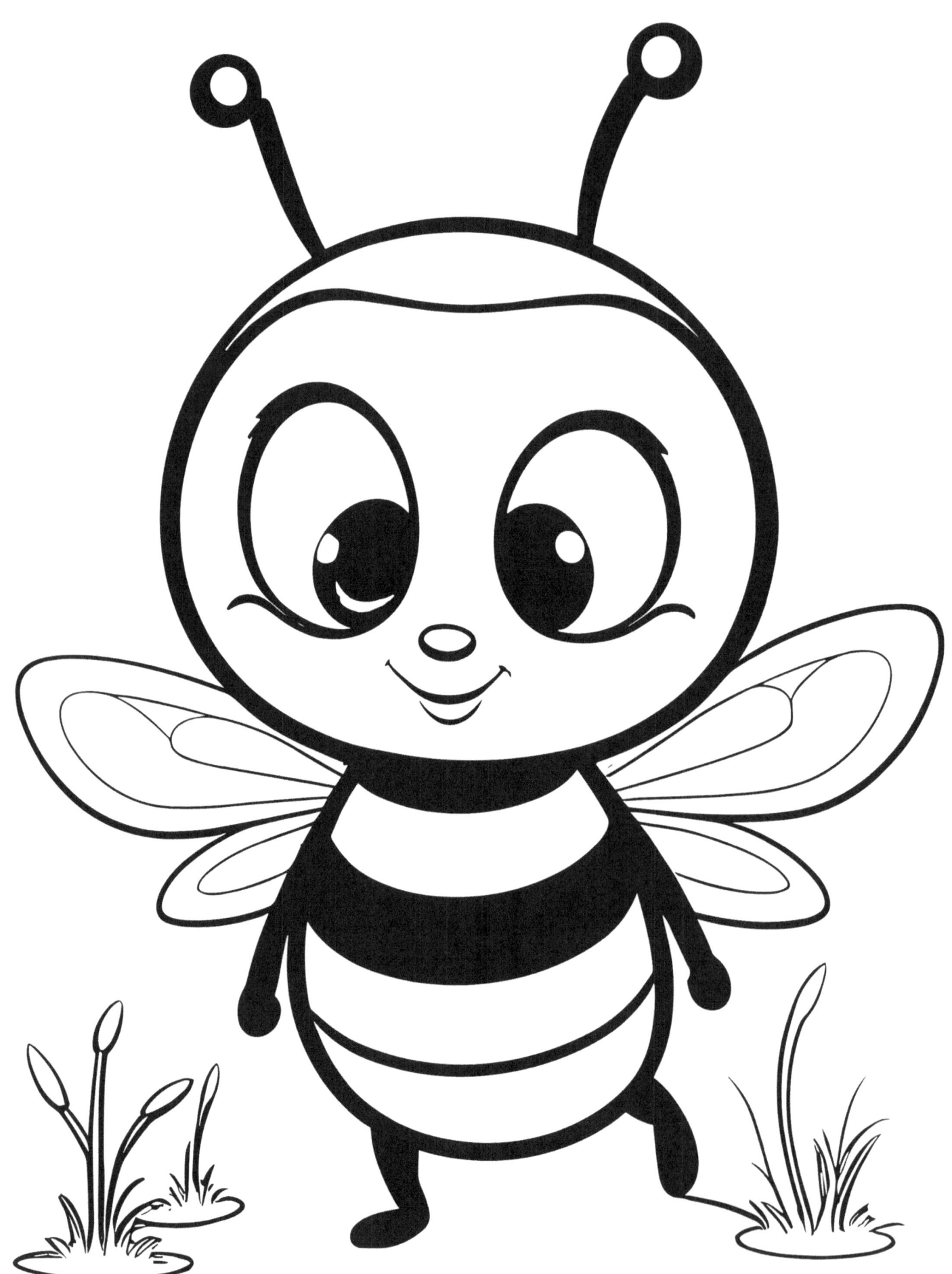

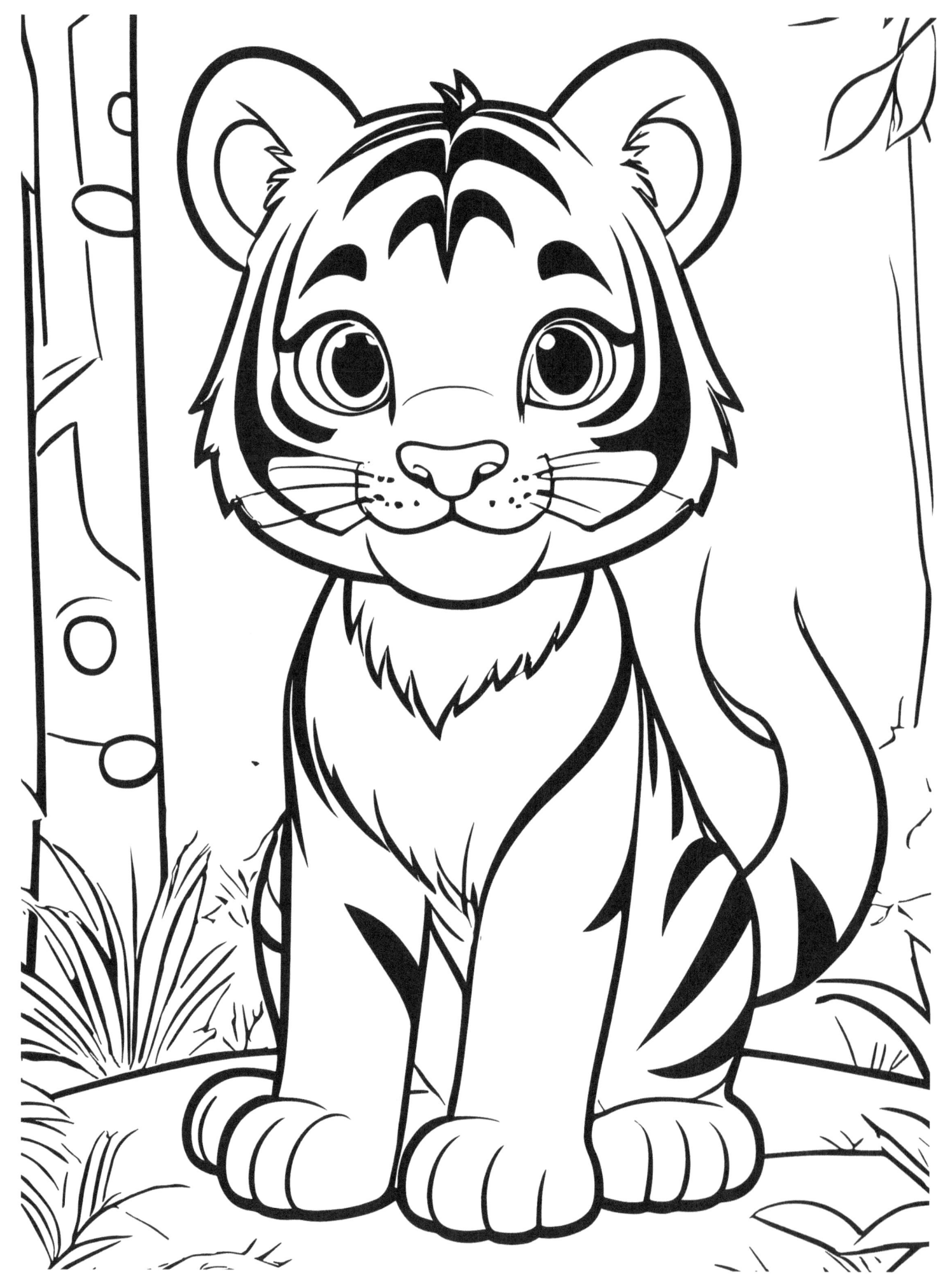

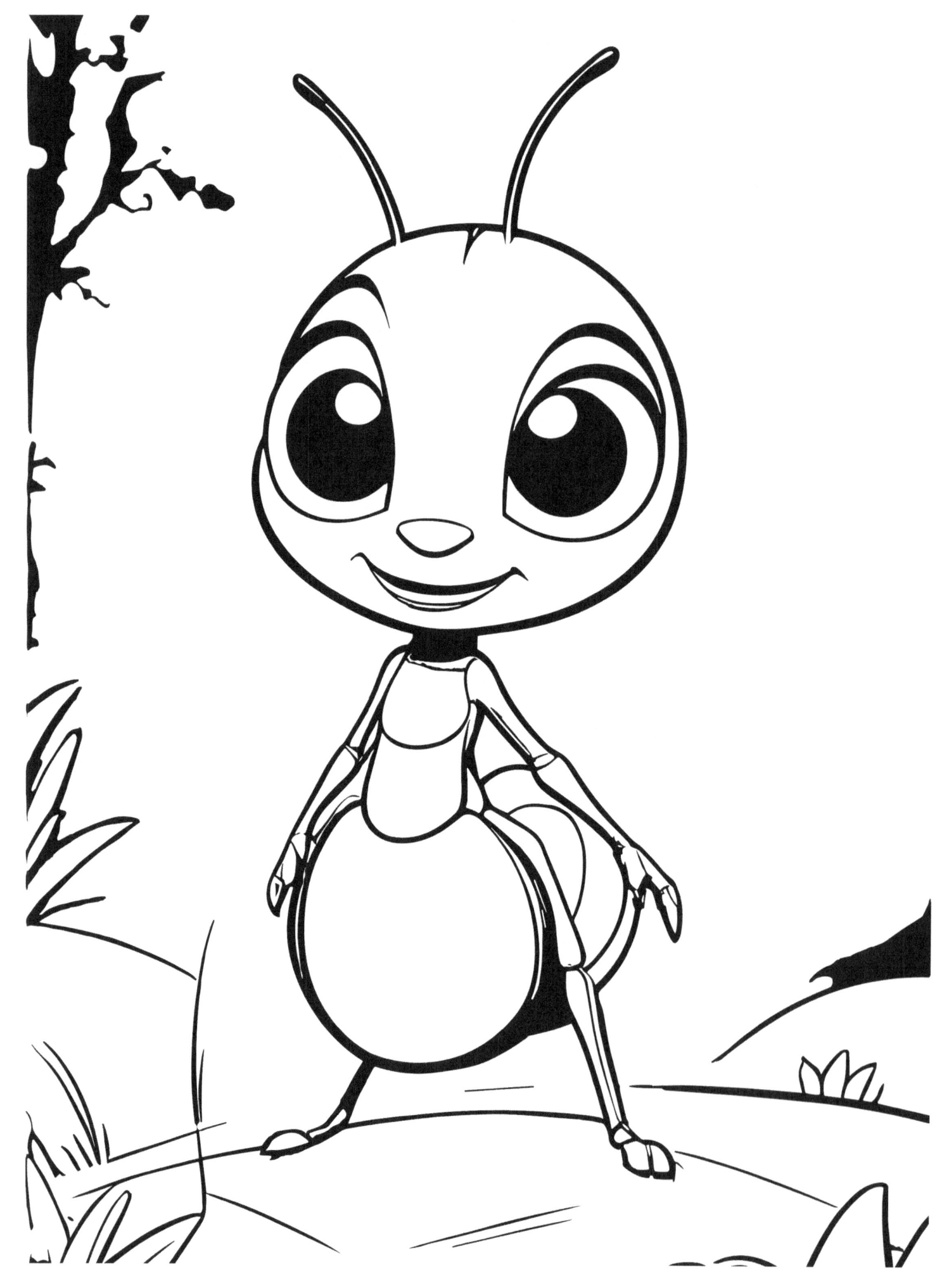

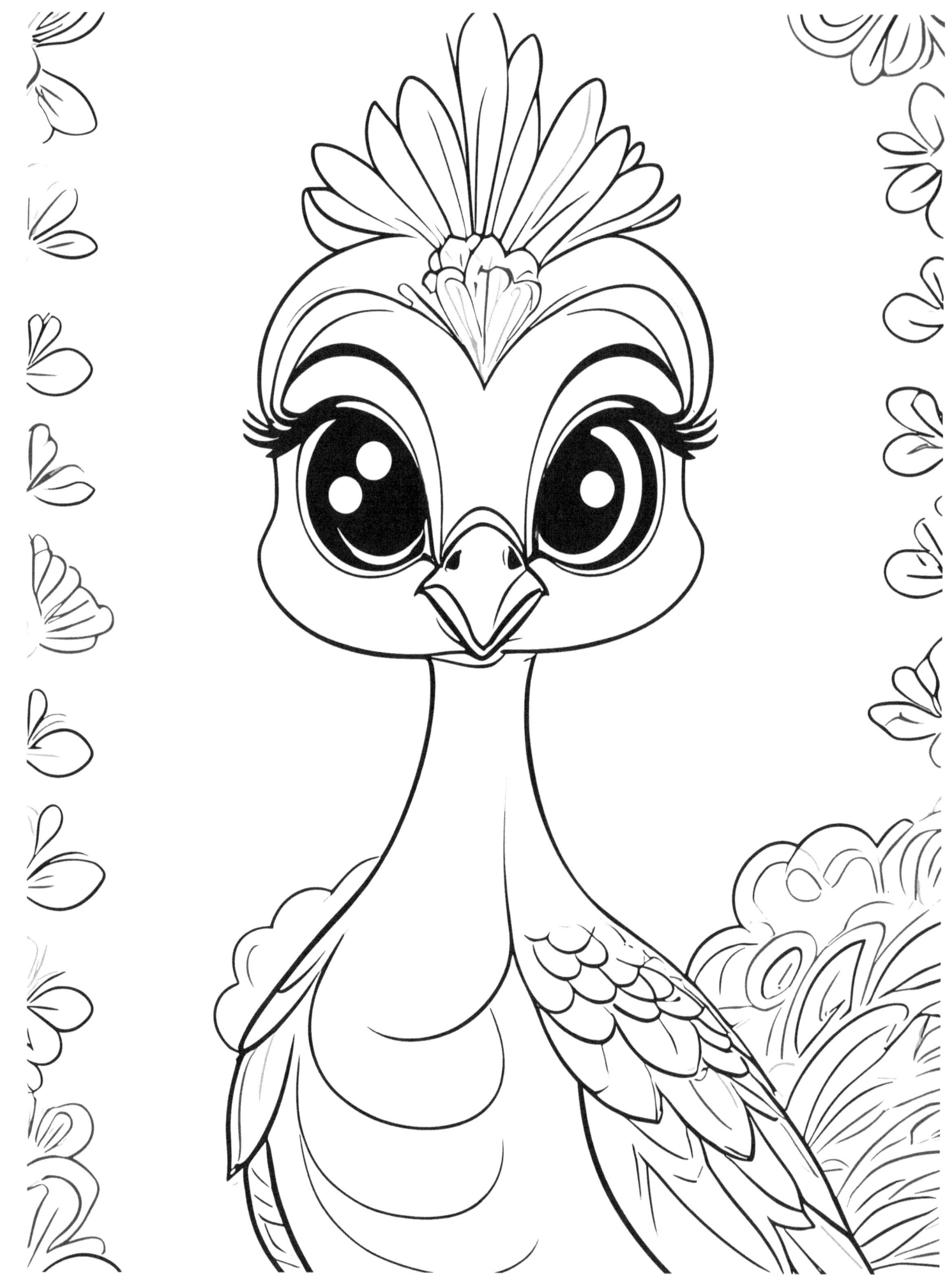

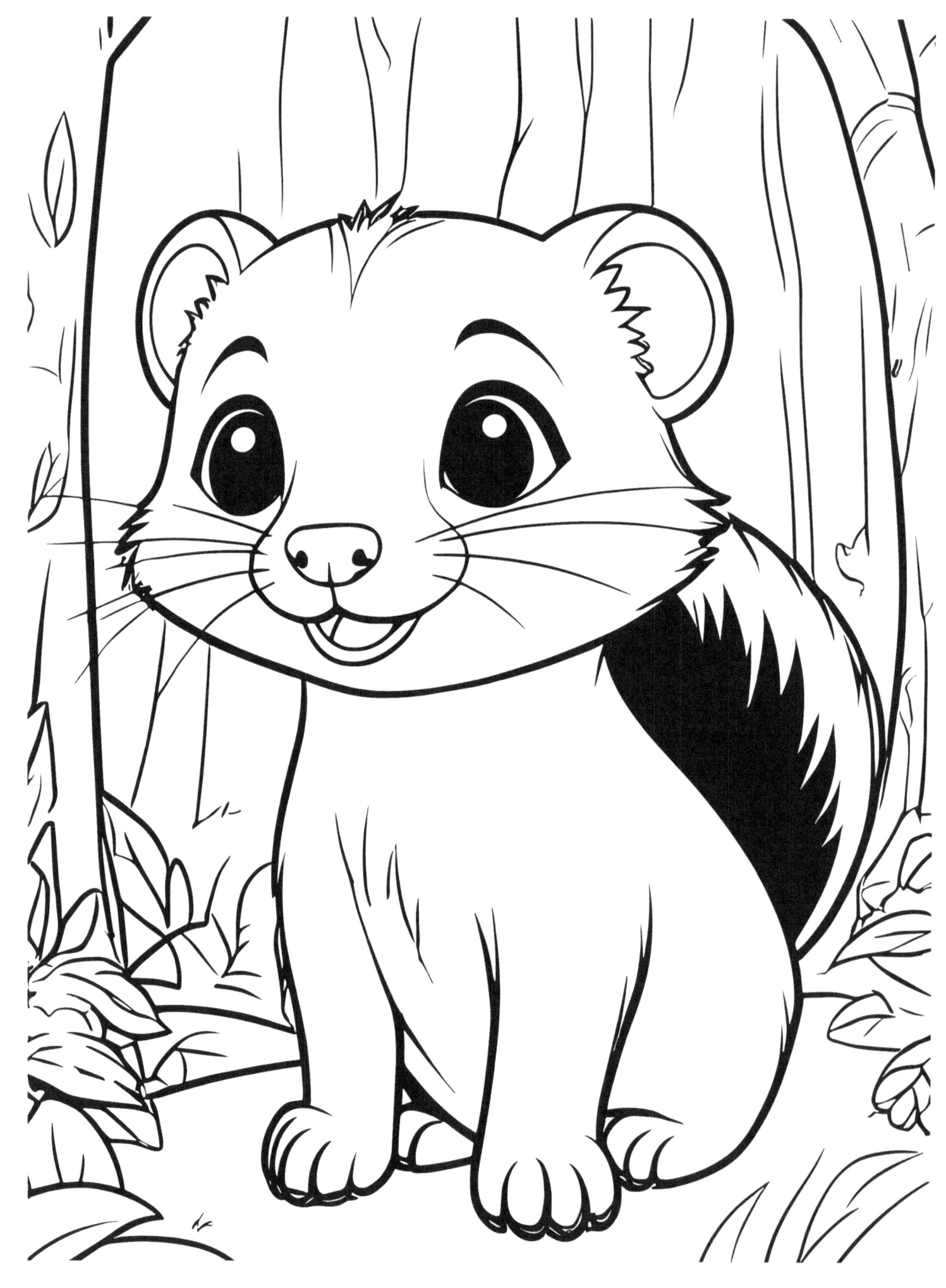

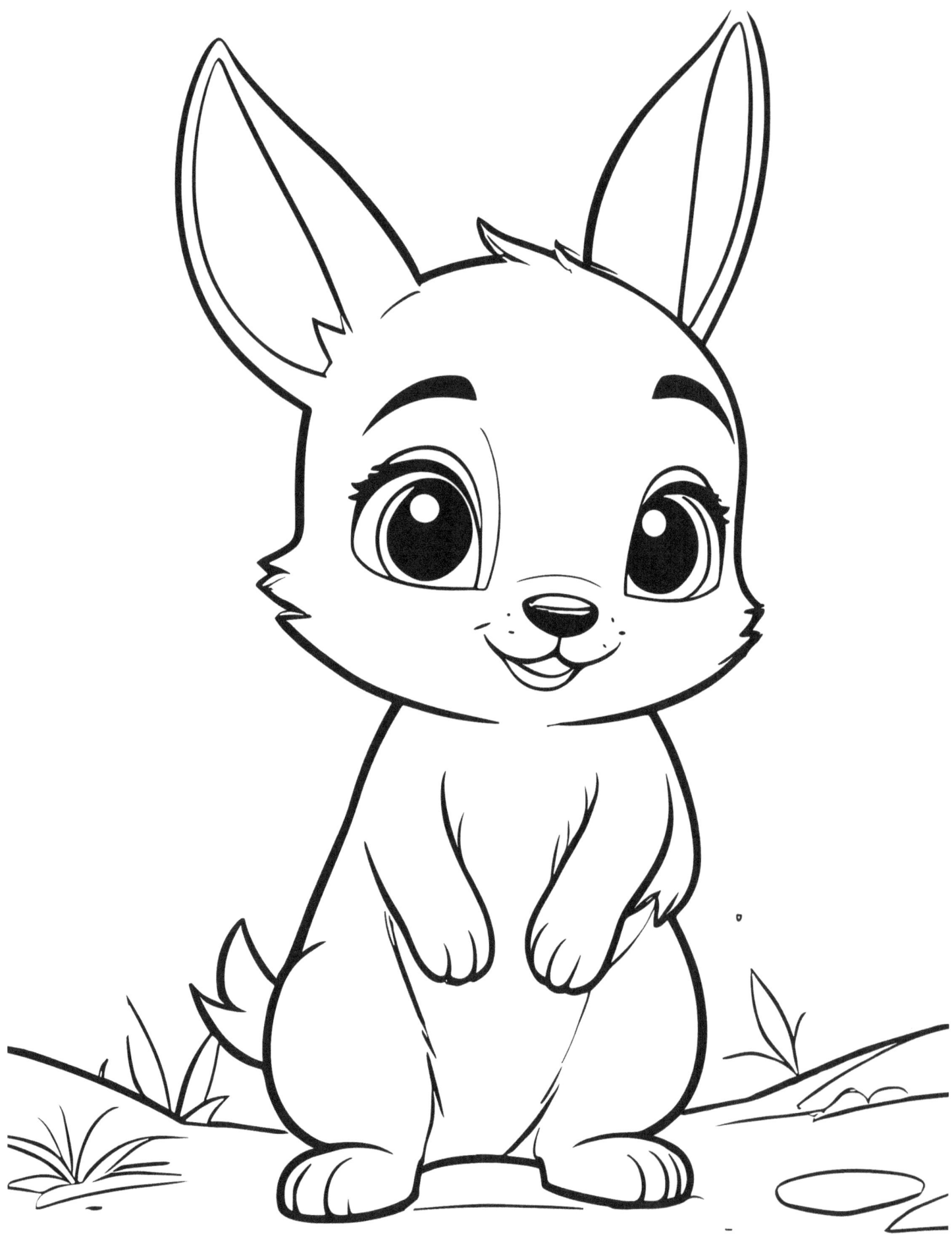

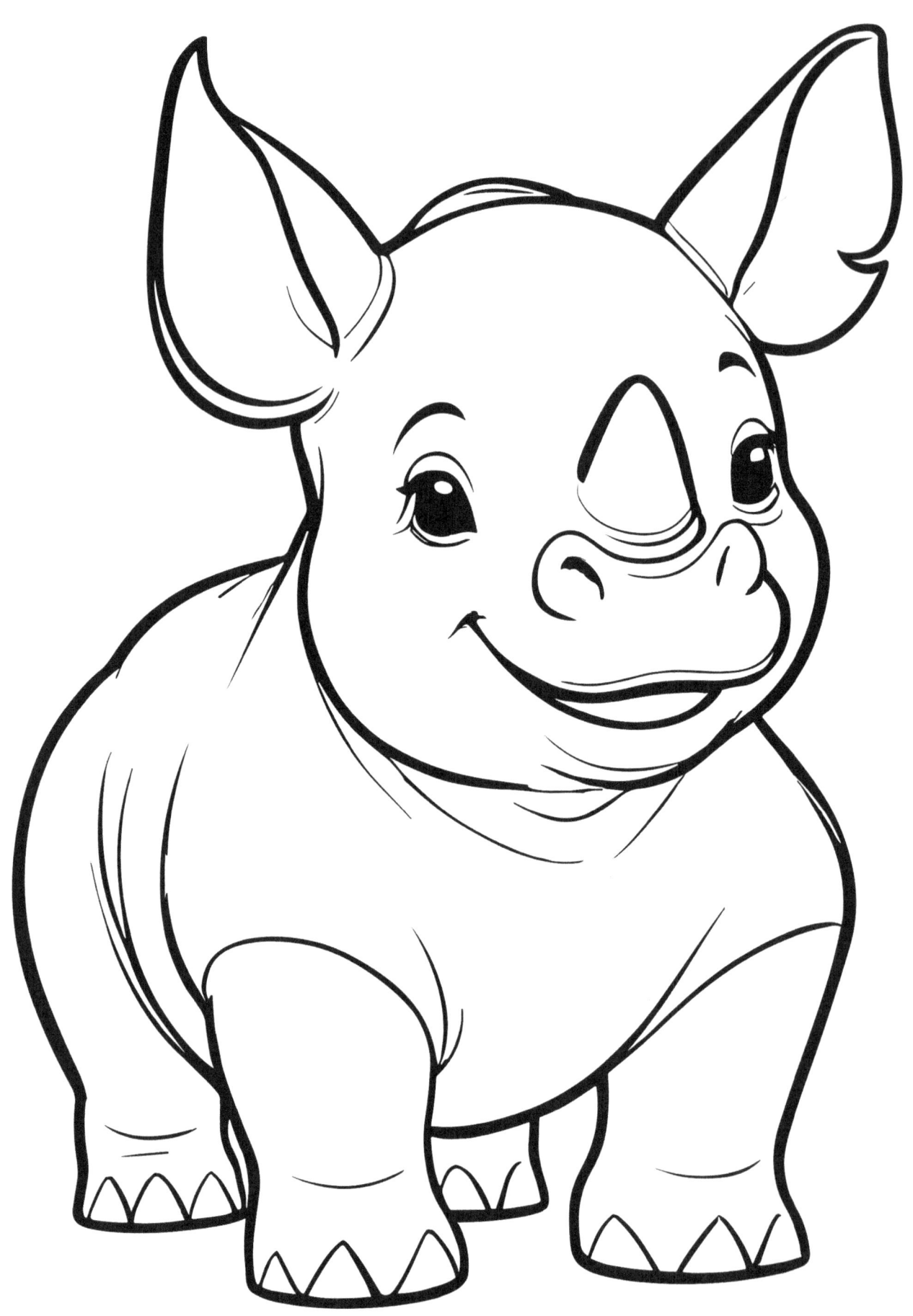

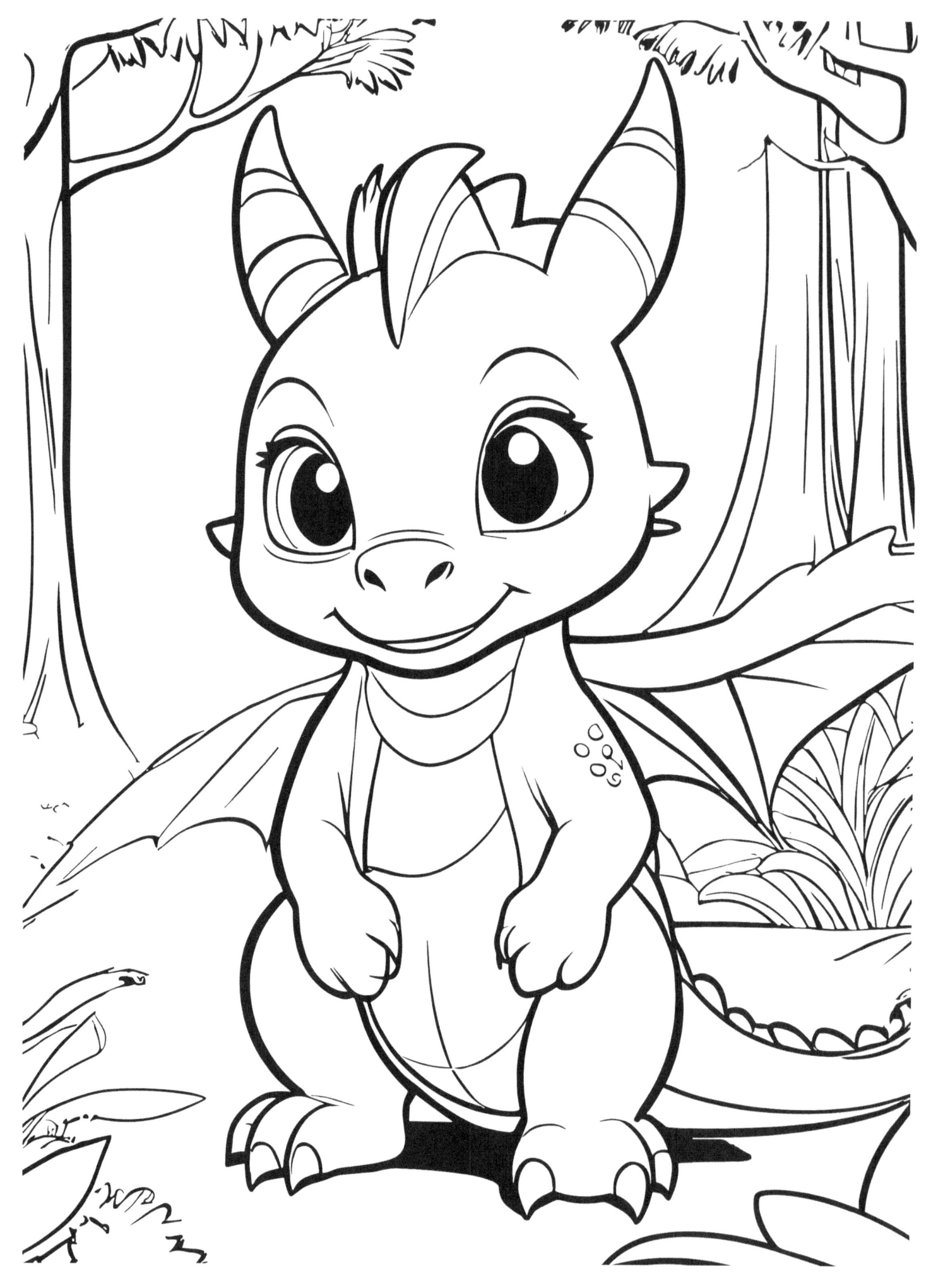

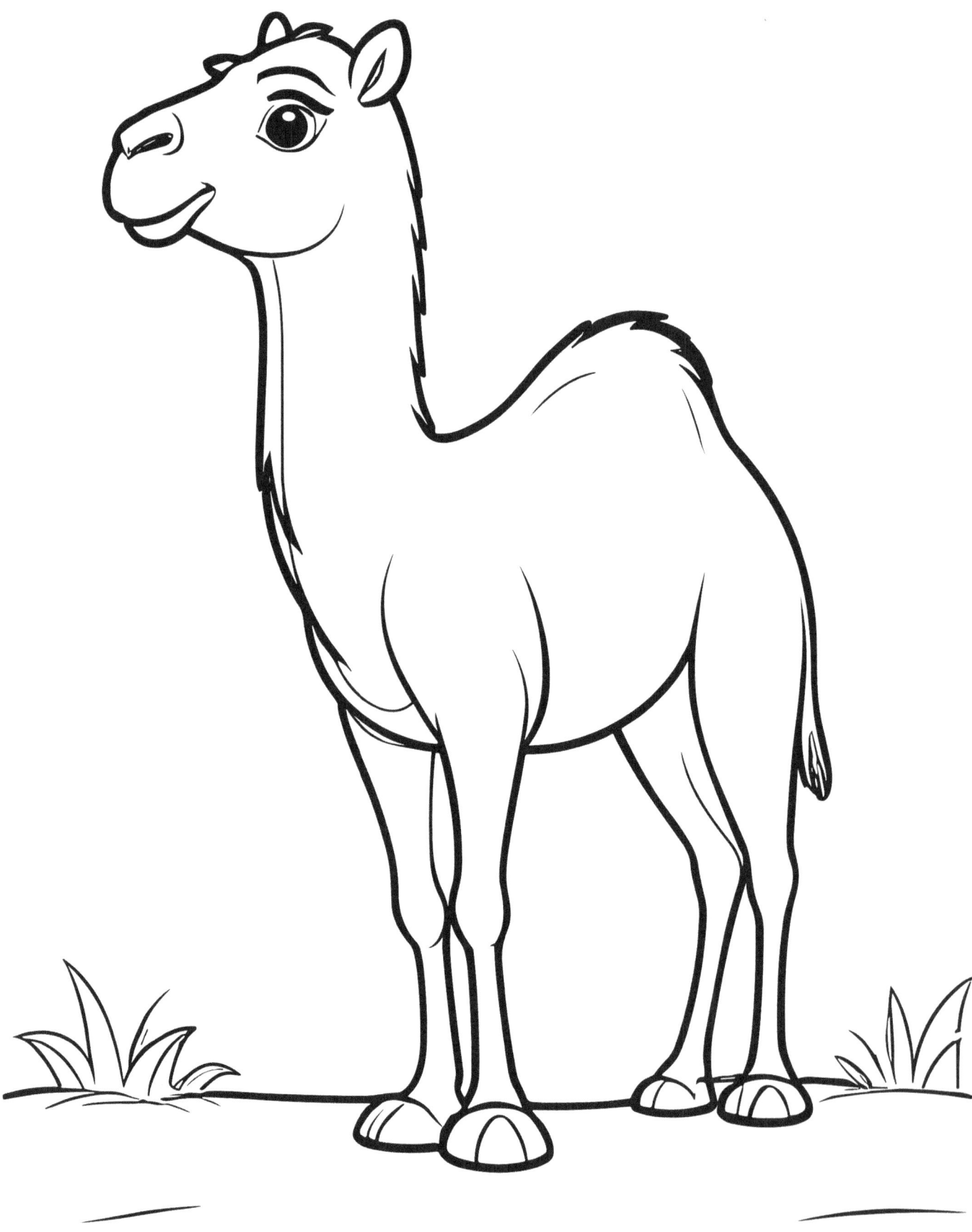

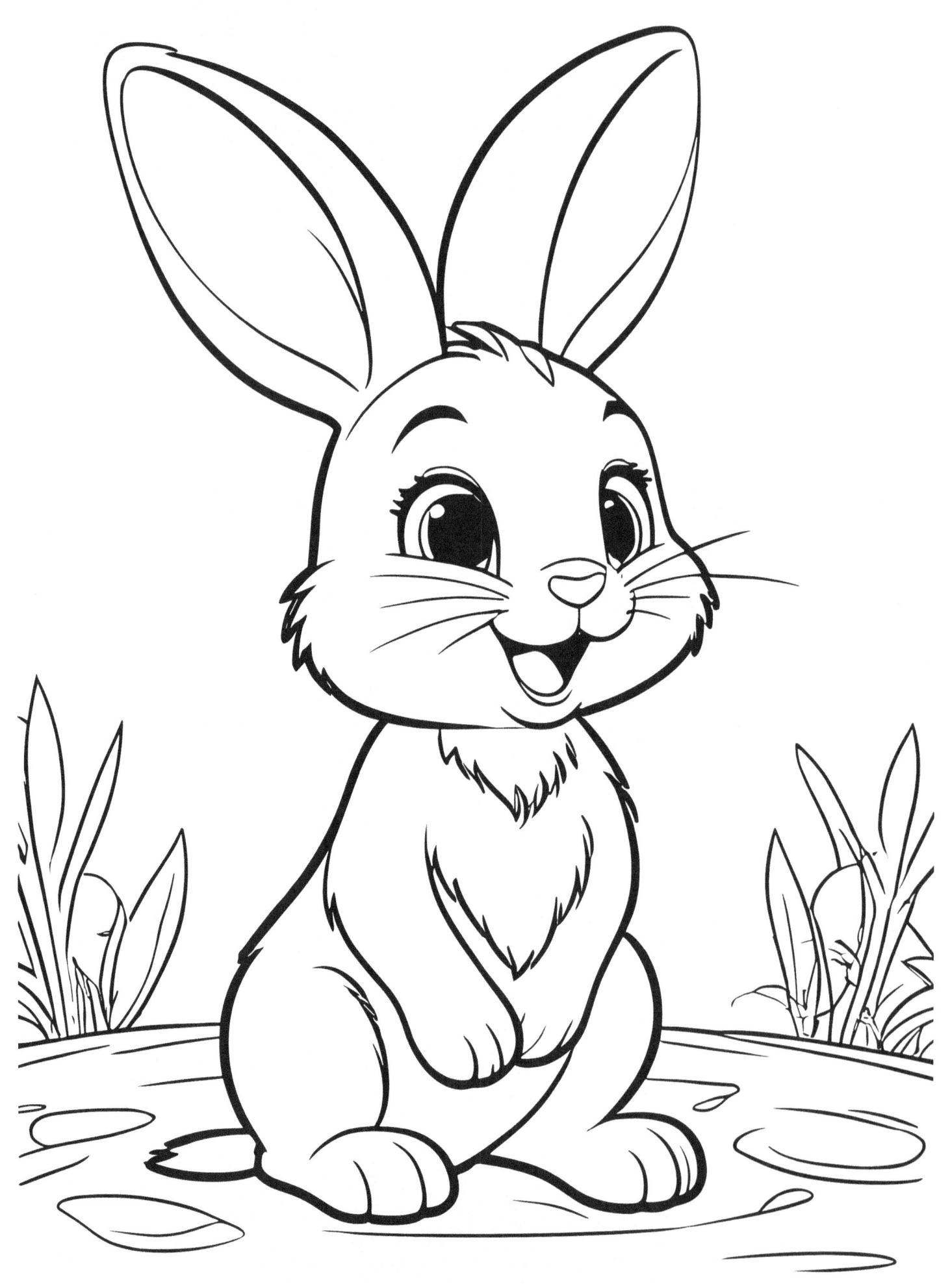

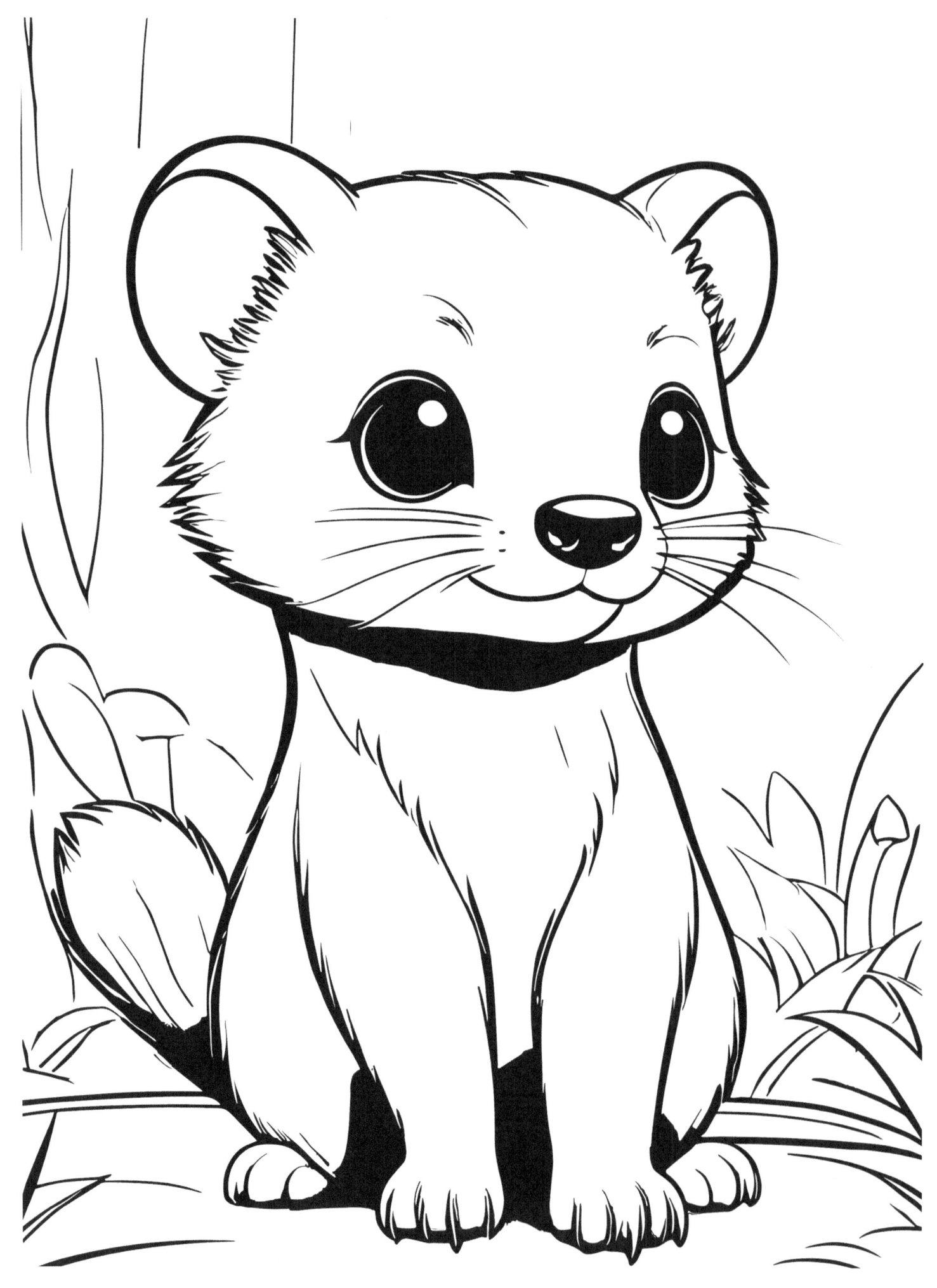

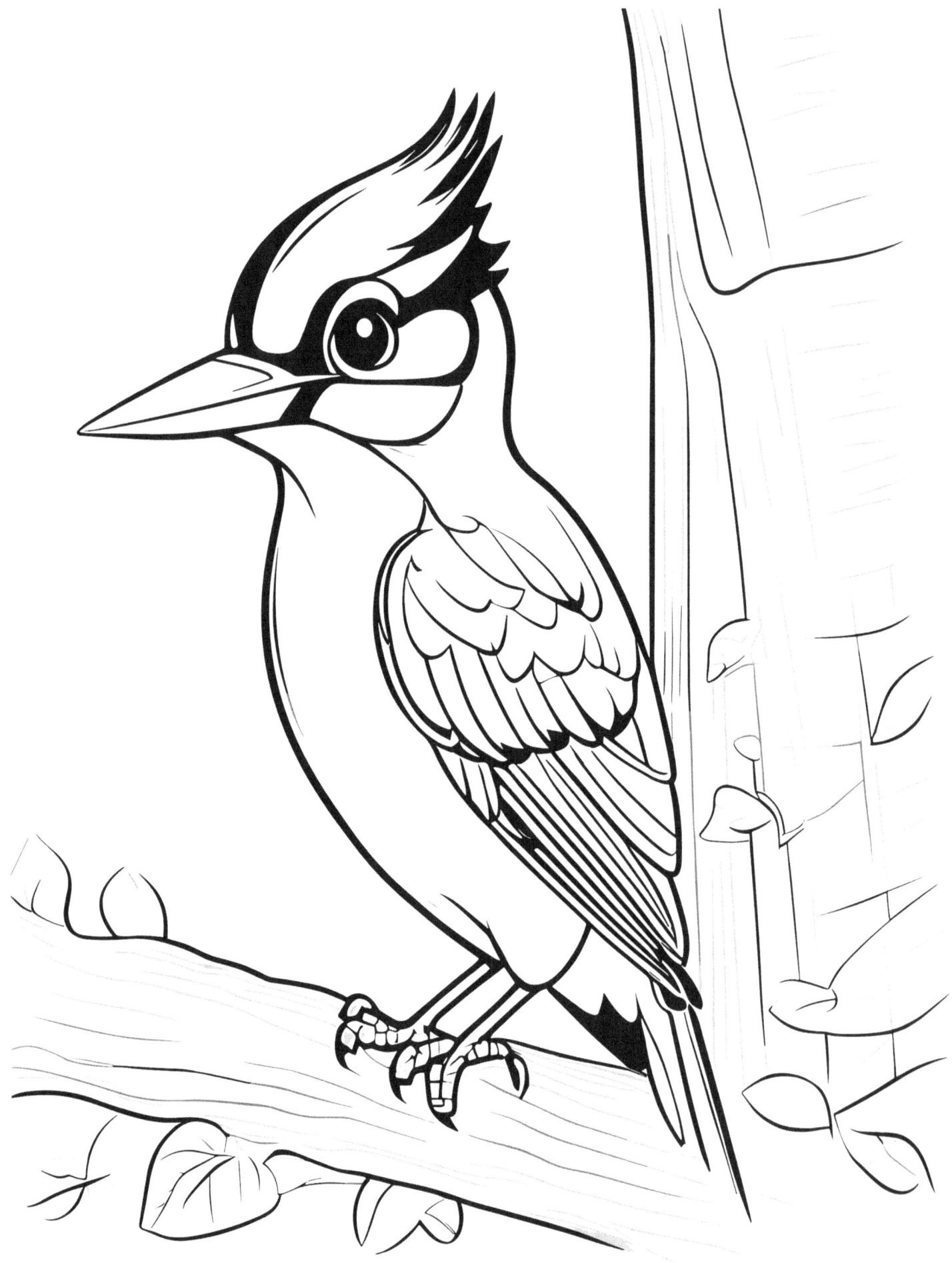

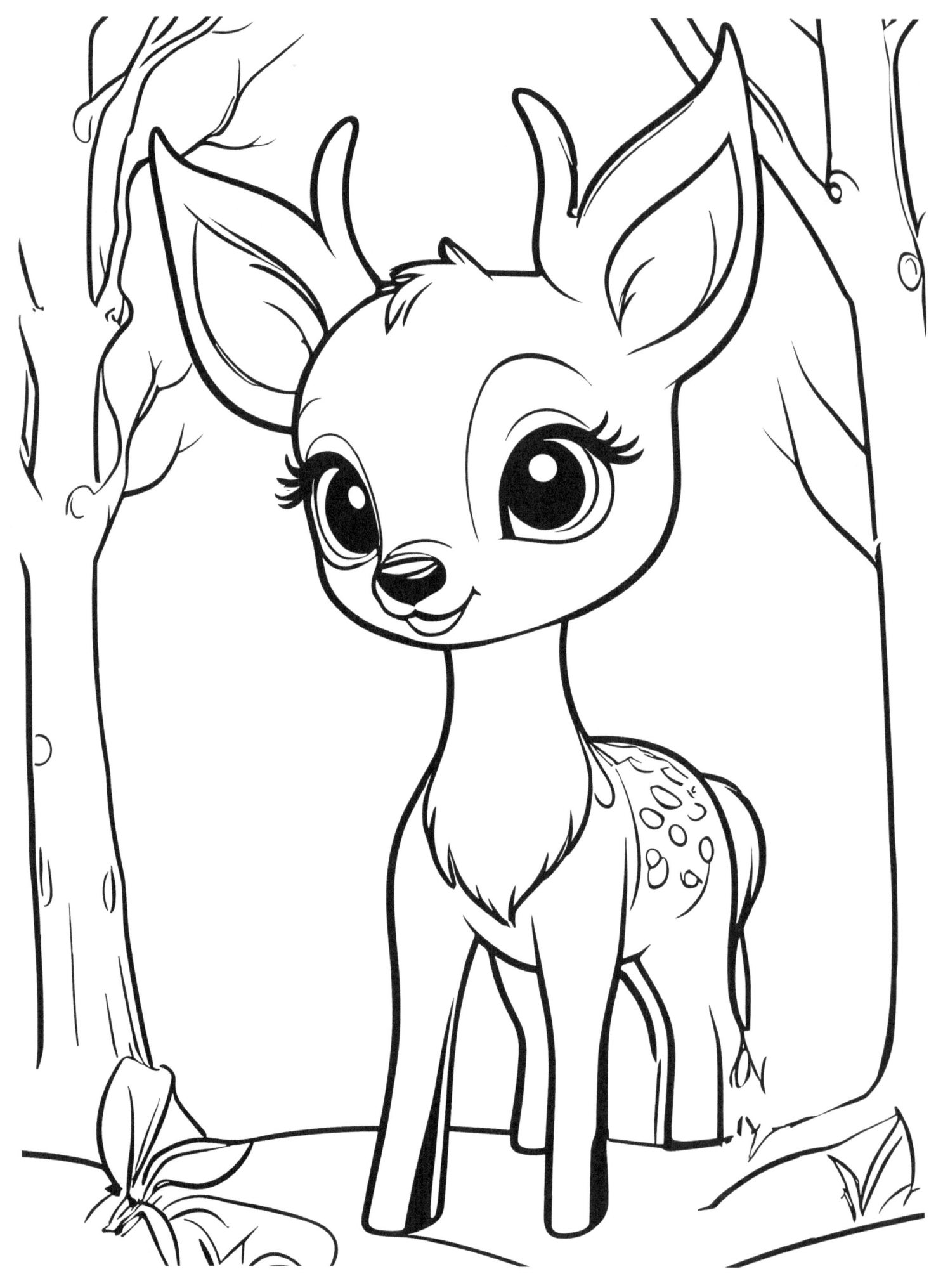

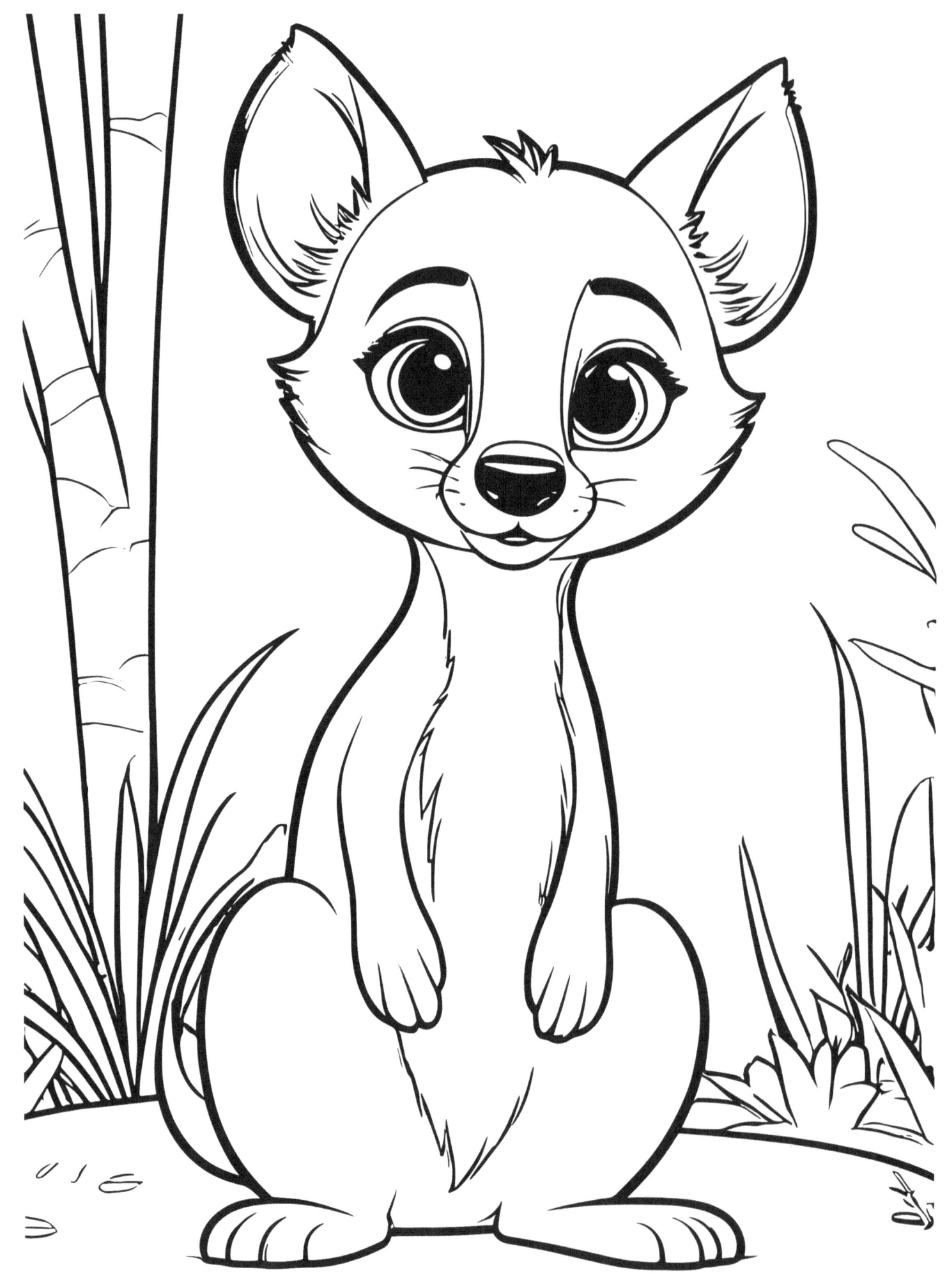

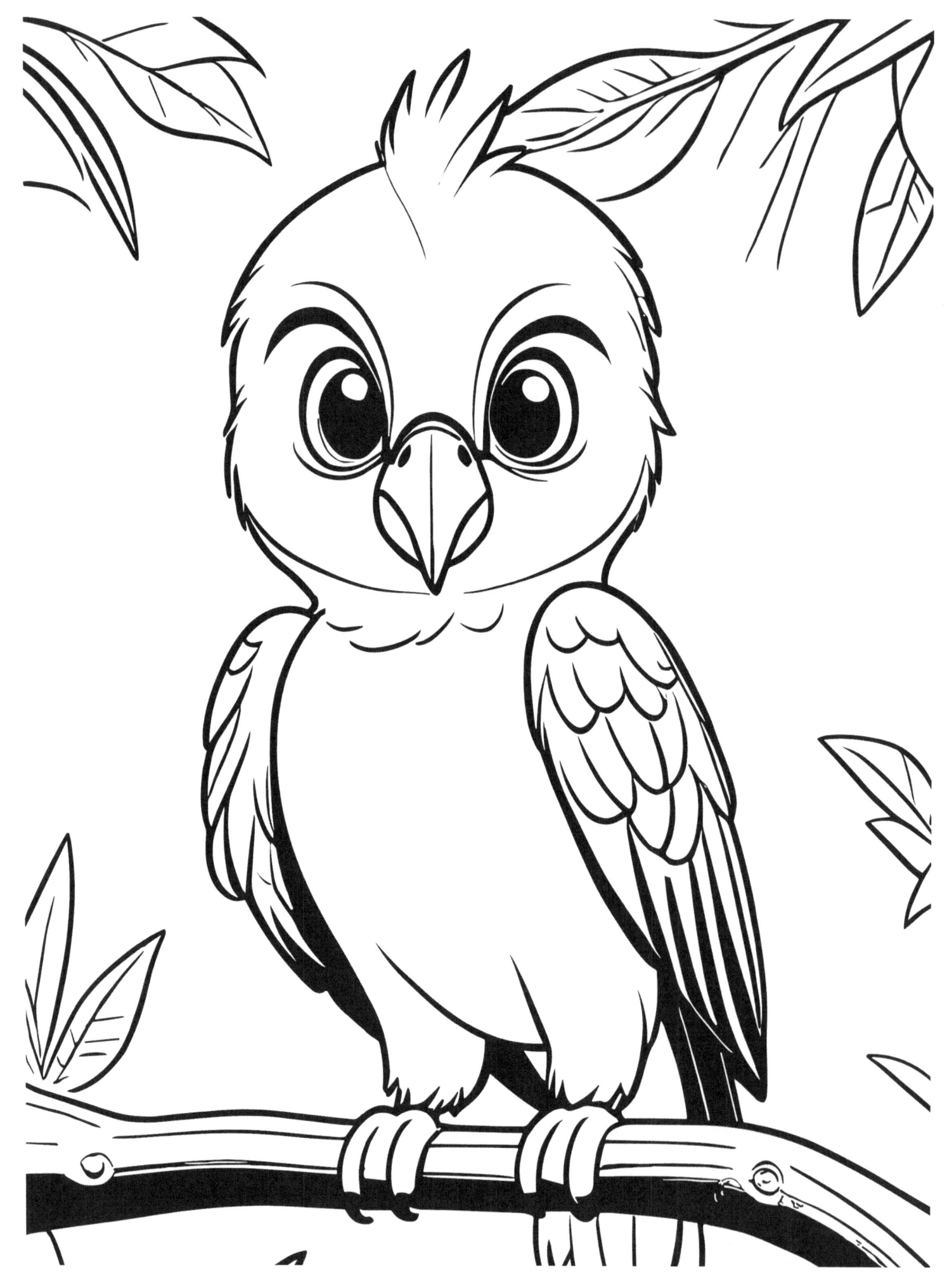